Left-Handed DADGAD and Dropped-D Photo Chords

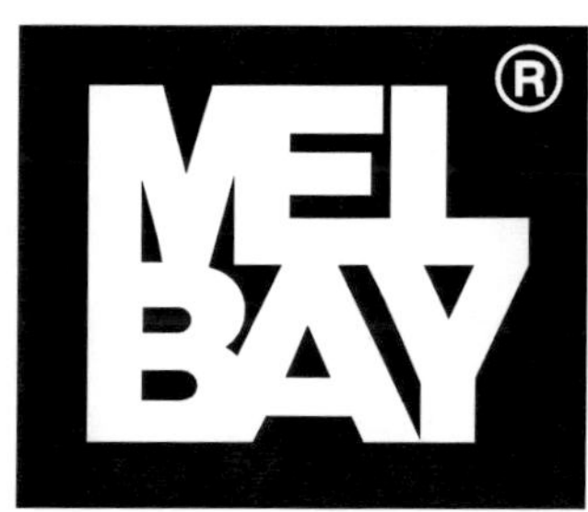

WWW.MELBAY.COM

DADGAD Chords

Dropped-D Chords

DADGAD

Tuning: D A D G A D

Strings: ⑥ ⑤ ④ ③ ② ①

D

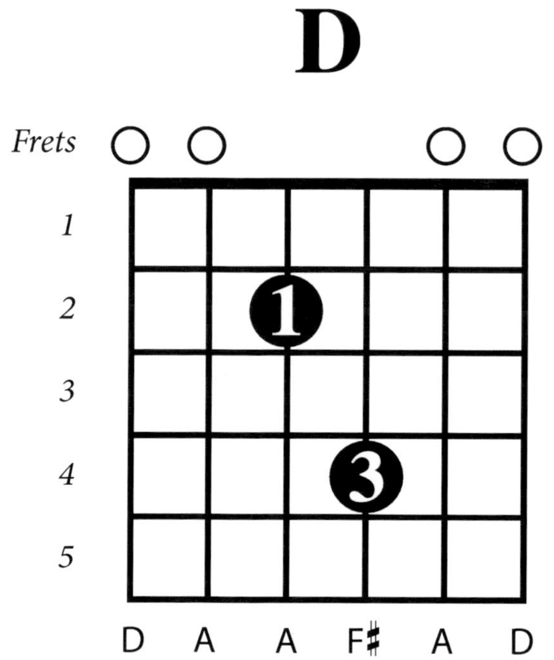

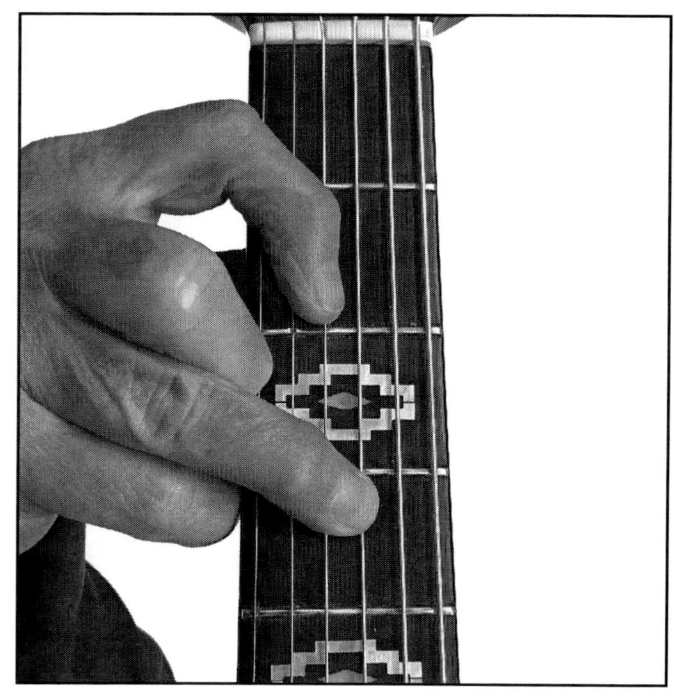

Dm

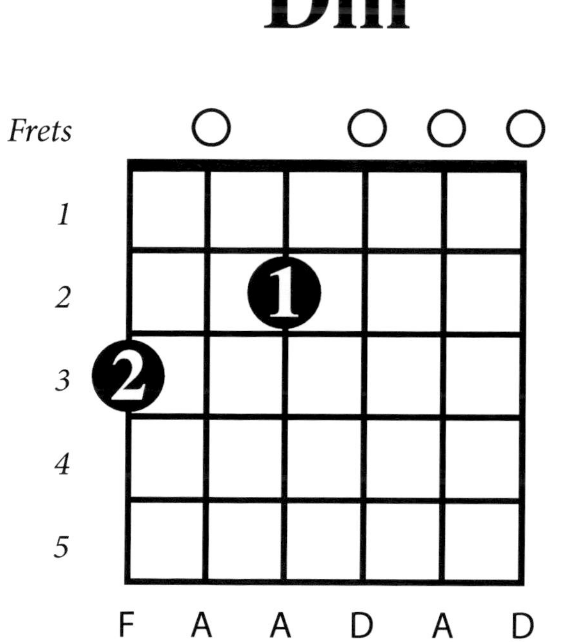

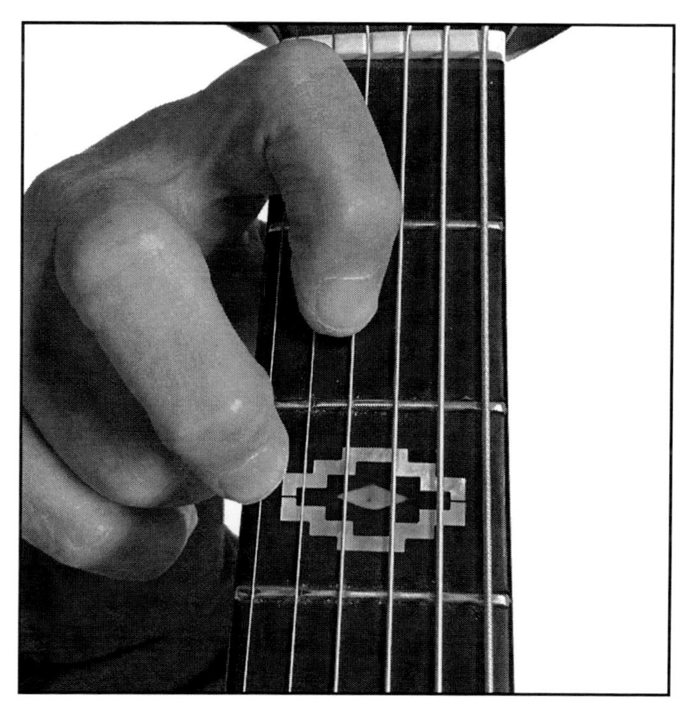

DADGAD

Tuning: **D A D G A D**
Strings: ⑥ ⑤ ④ ③ ② ①

D7

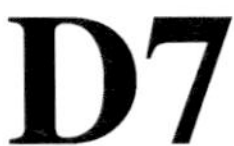

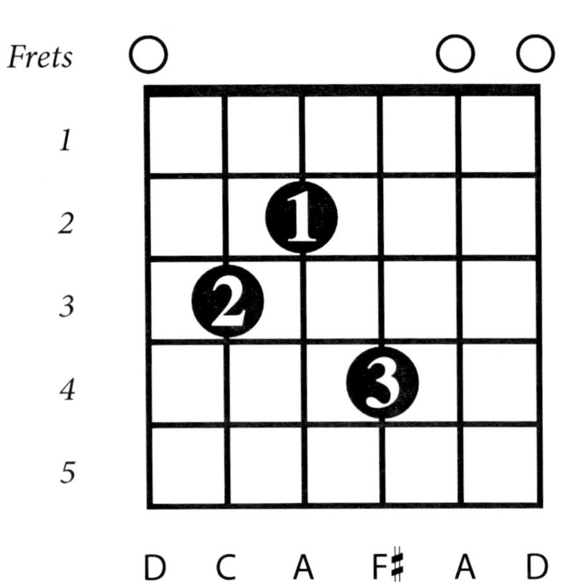

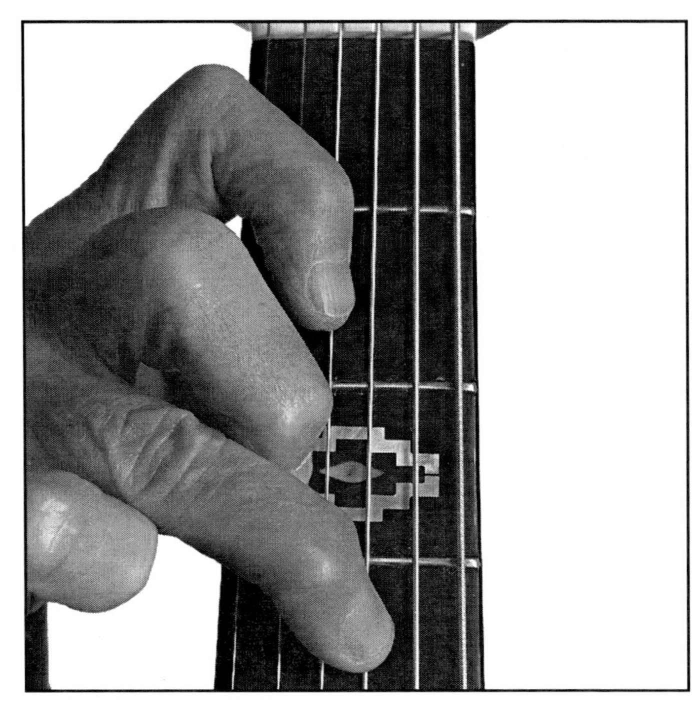

DMaj7

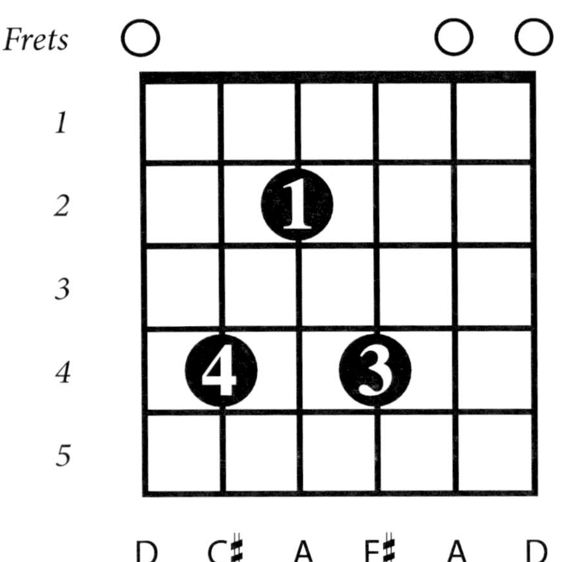

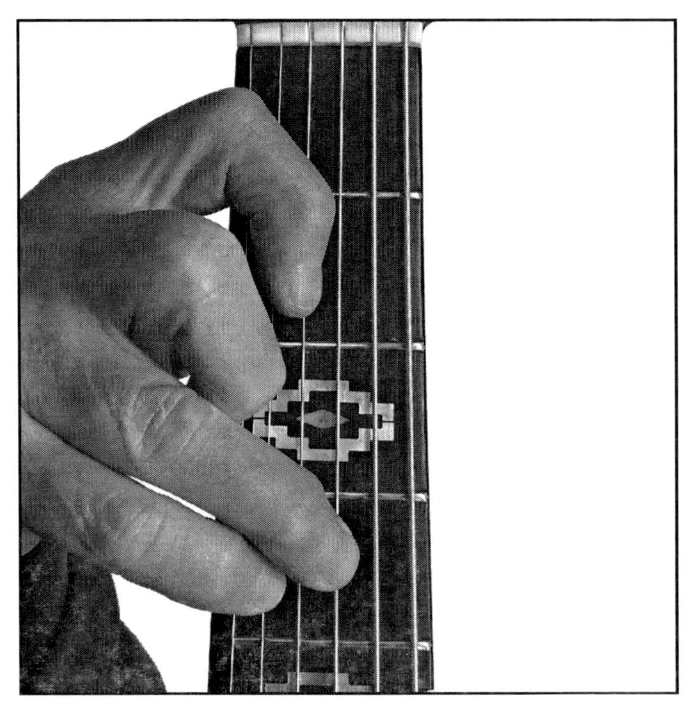

DADGAD

Tuning: **D A D G A D**
Strings: ⑥ ⑤ ④ ③ ② ①

DMaj6

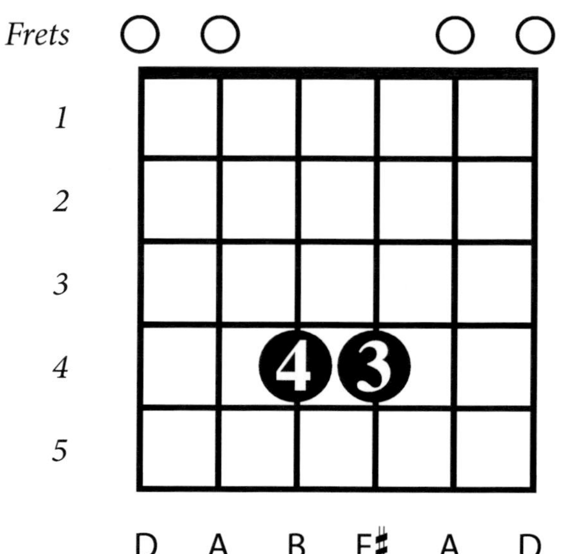

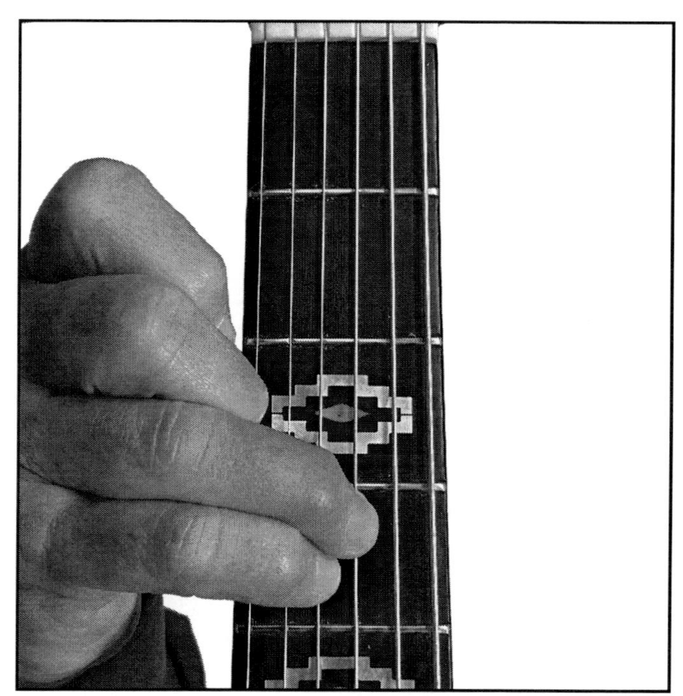

Dm6

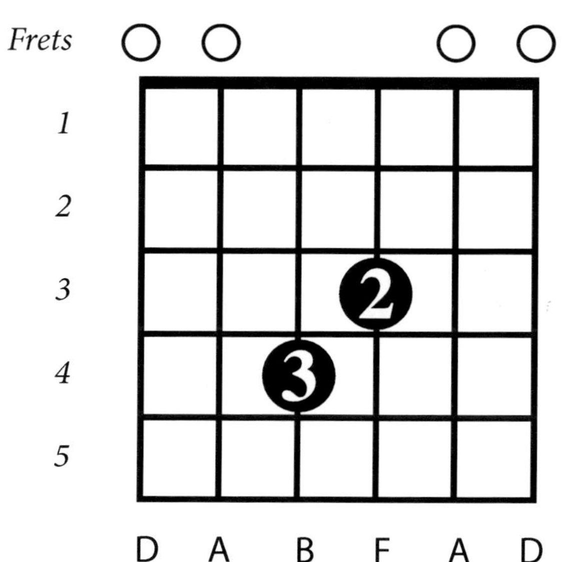

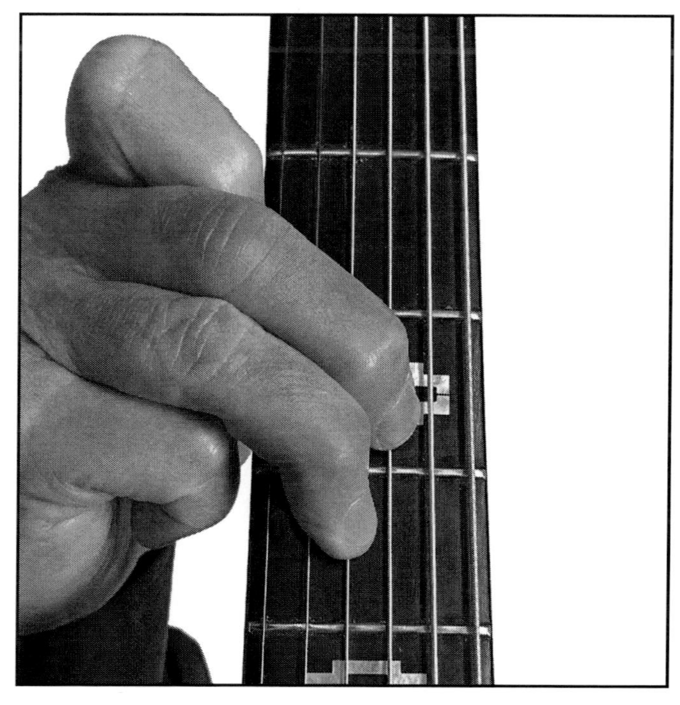

DADGAD

Tuning: **D A D G A D**

Strings: ⑥ ⑤ ④ ③ ② ①

Dm7

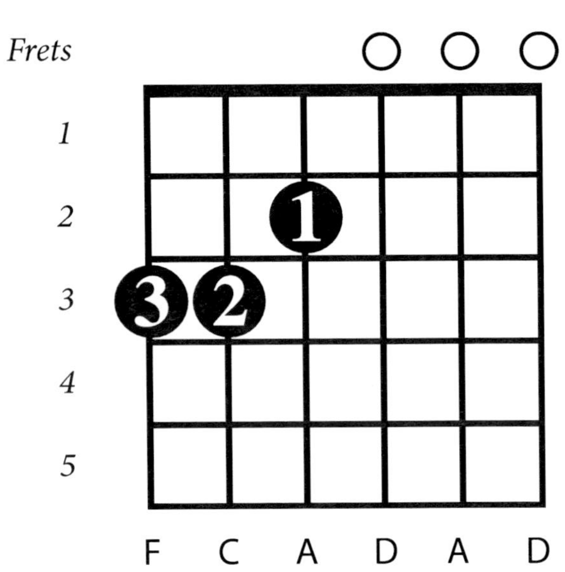

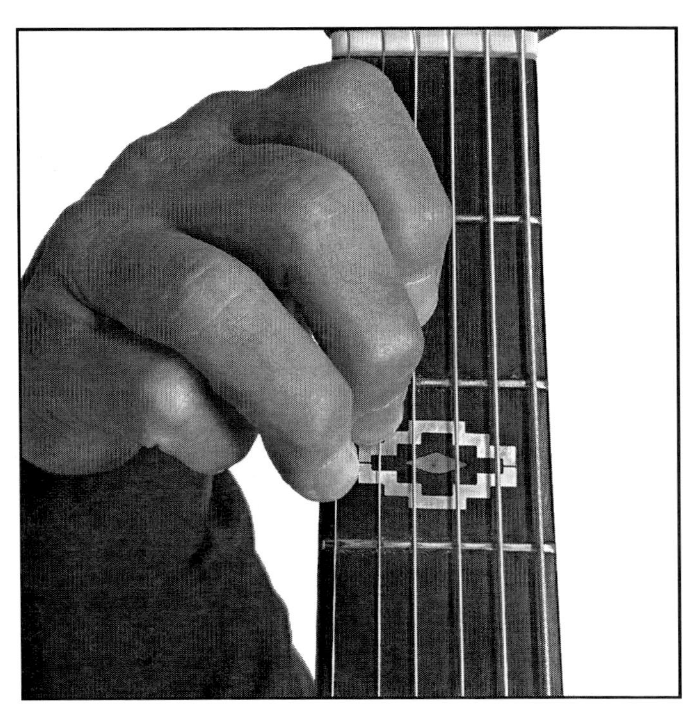

Dm-Maj7

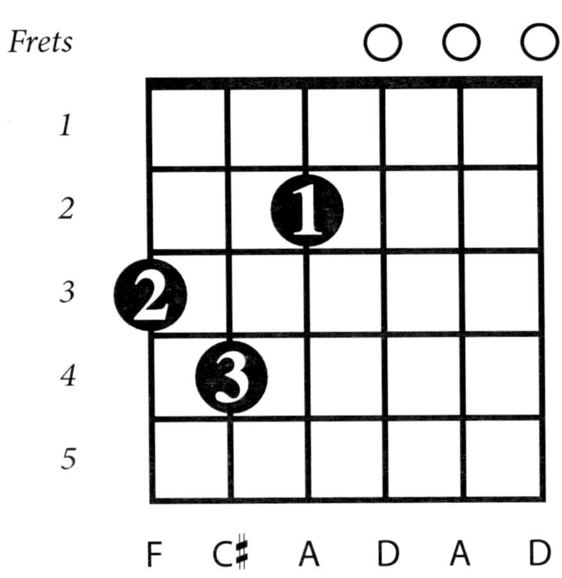

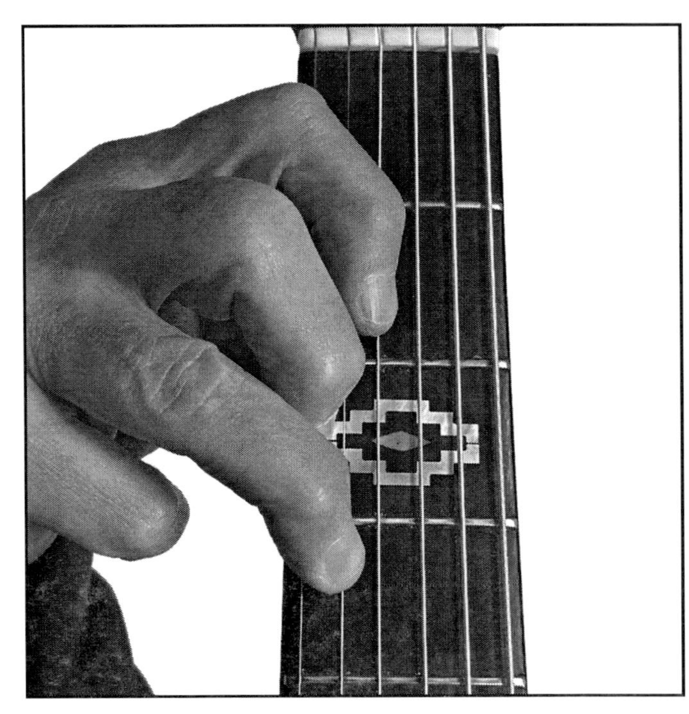

DADGAD

Tuning: **D A D G A D**
Strings: ⑥ ⑤ ④ ③ ② ①

D add9

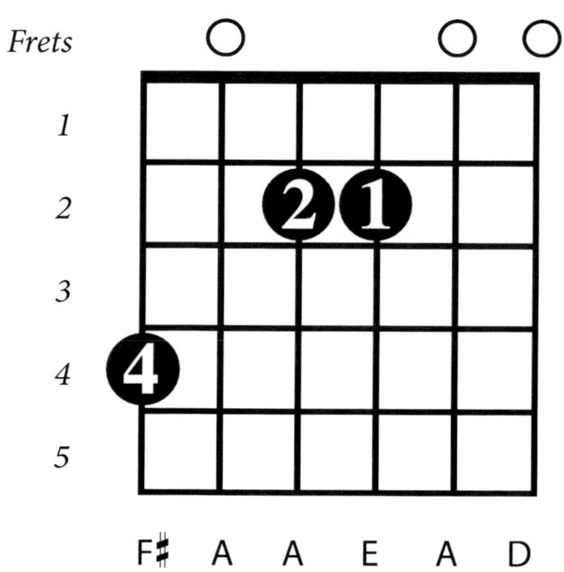

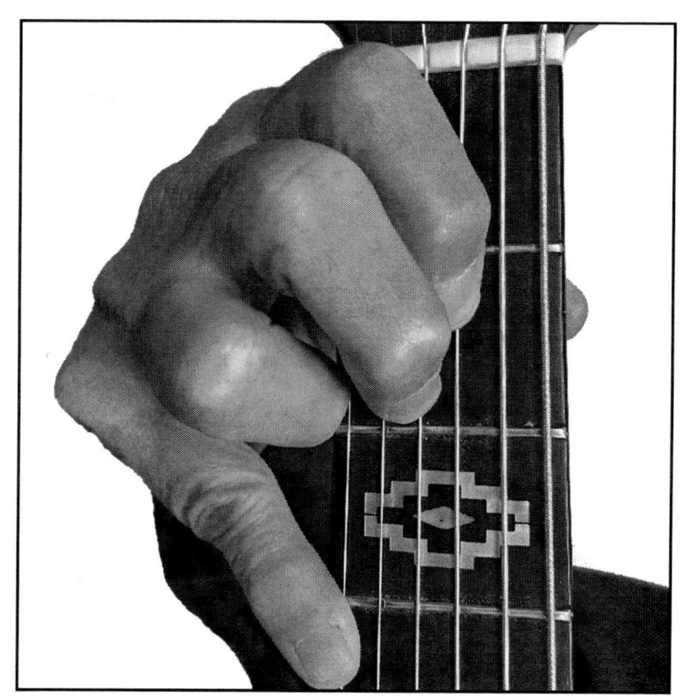

Dm add9

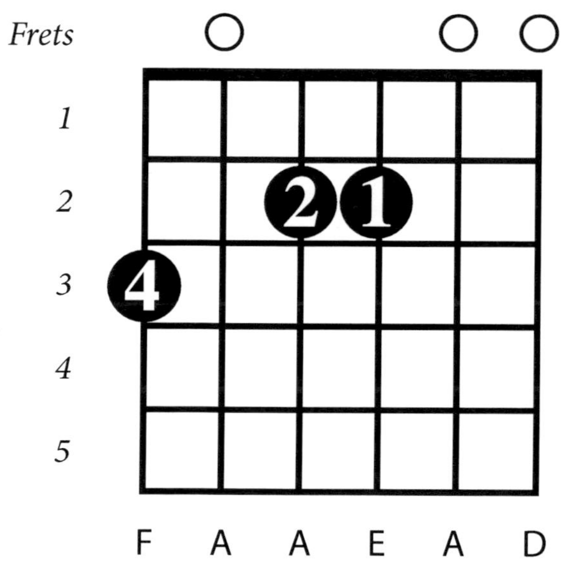

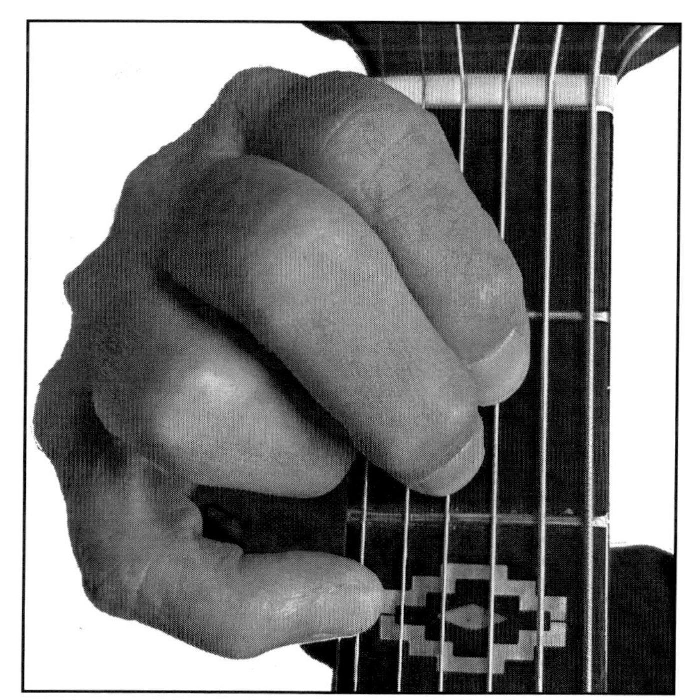

DADGAD

Tuning: **D A D G A D**
Strings: ⑥ ⑤ ④ ③ ② ①

Dsus

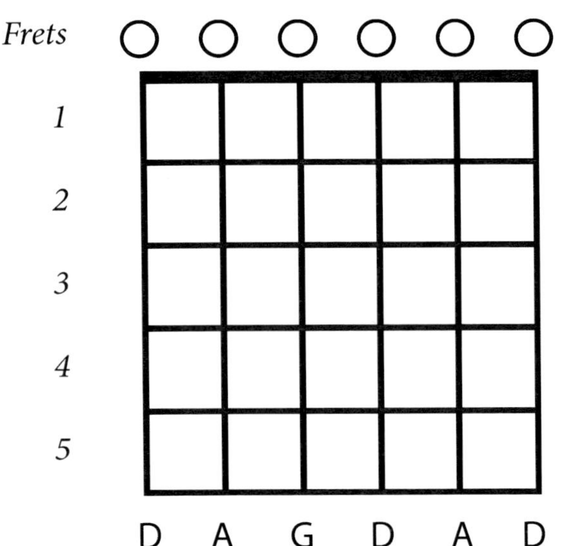

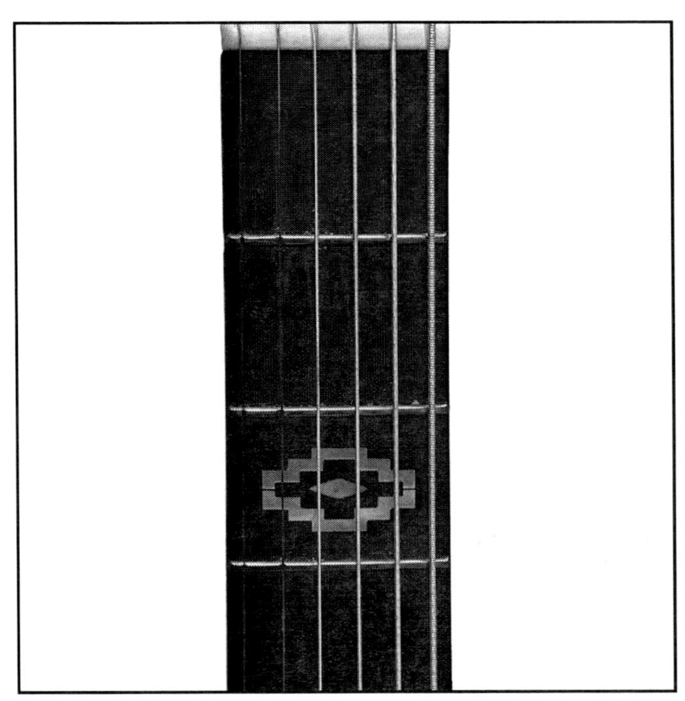

DMaj7 add6

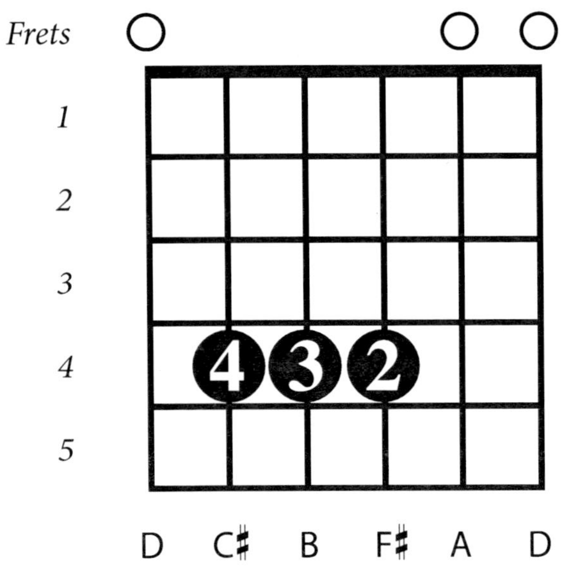

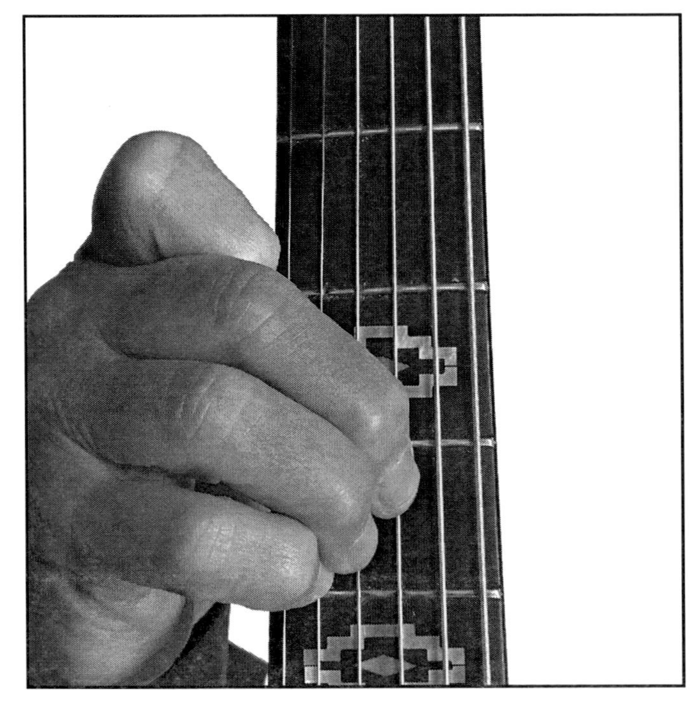

DADGAD

Tuning: **D A D G A D**
Strings: ⑥ ⑤ ④ ③ ② ①

DMaj9

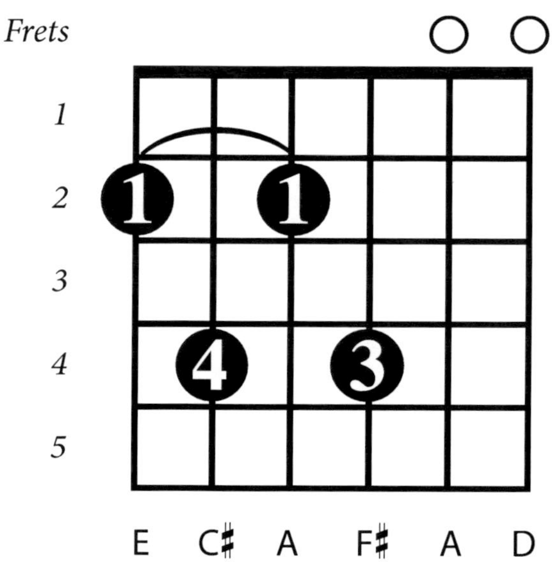

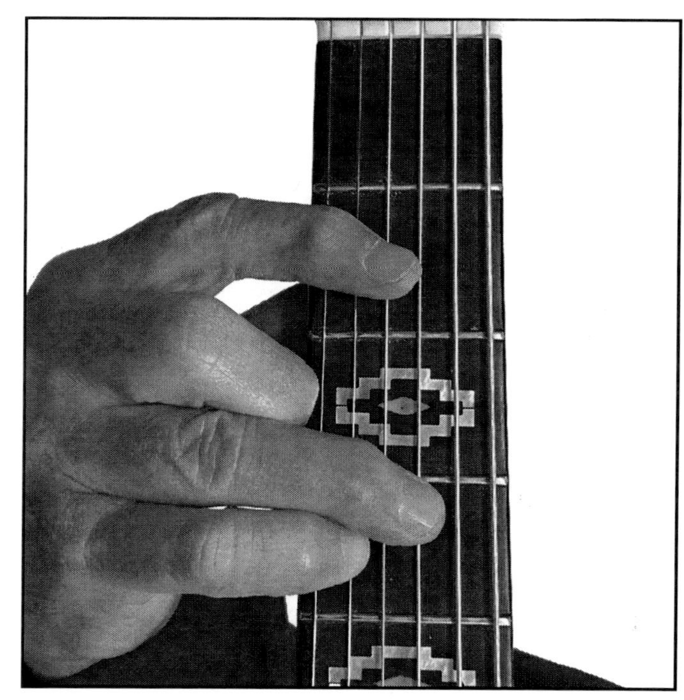

DMaj13

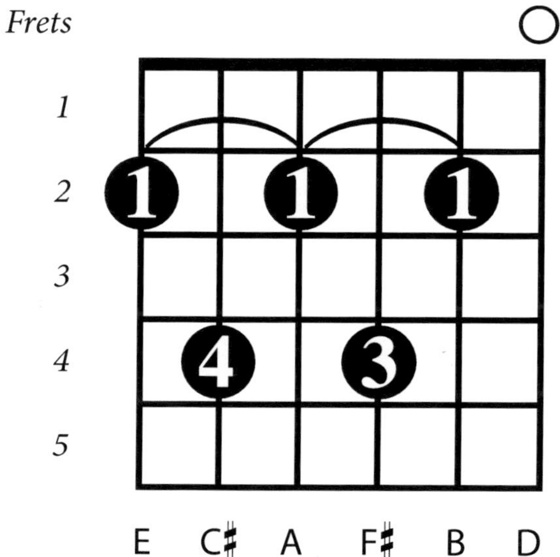

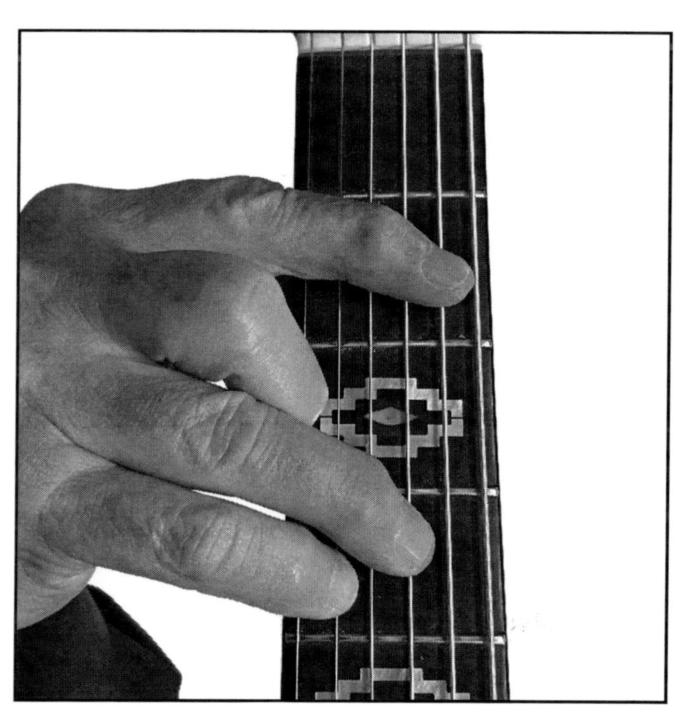

DADGAD

Tuning: **D A D G A D**

Strings: ⑥ ⑤ ④ ③ ② ①

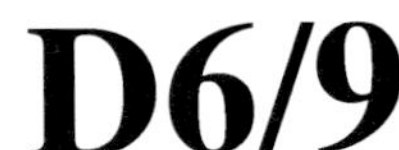

D6/9

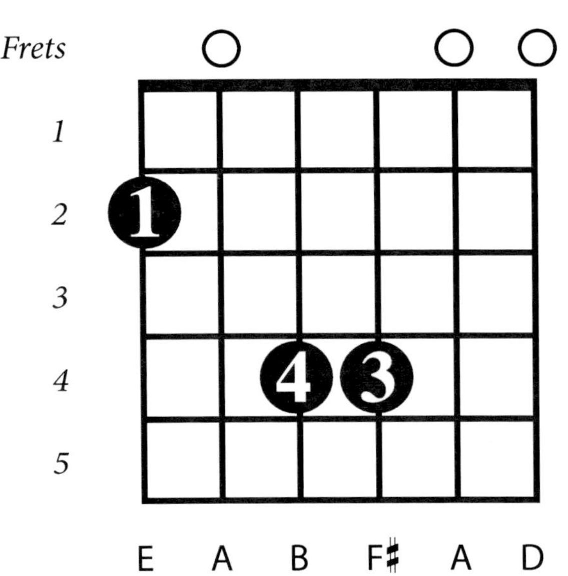

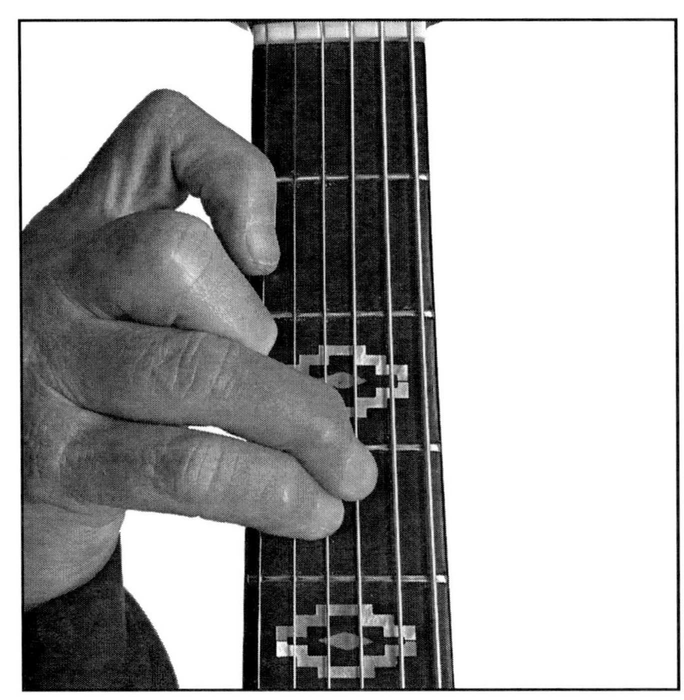

D°

Frets

1
2
3
4
5

D B A♭ F B D
(C♭)

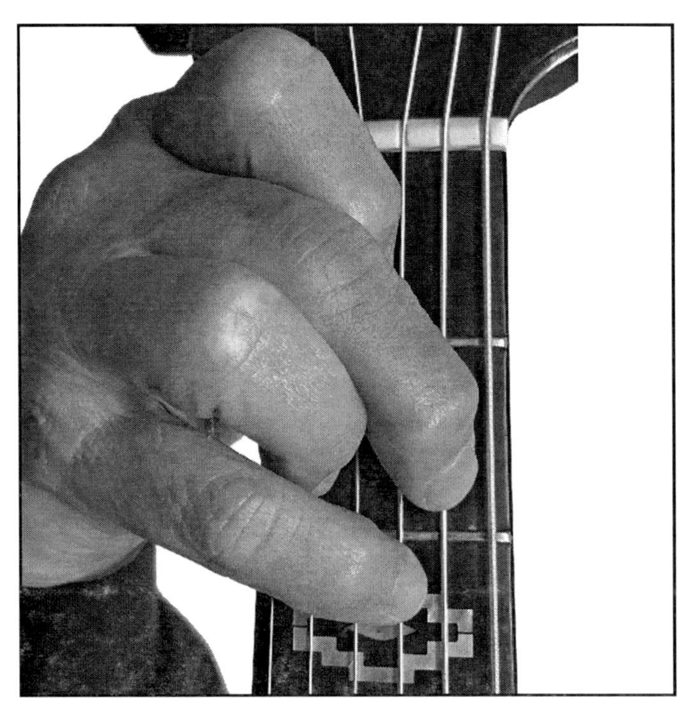

DADGAD

Tuning: **D A D G A D**
Strings: ⑥ ⑤ ④ ③ ② ①

Em

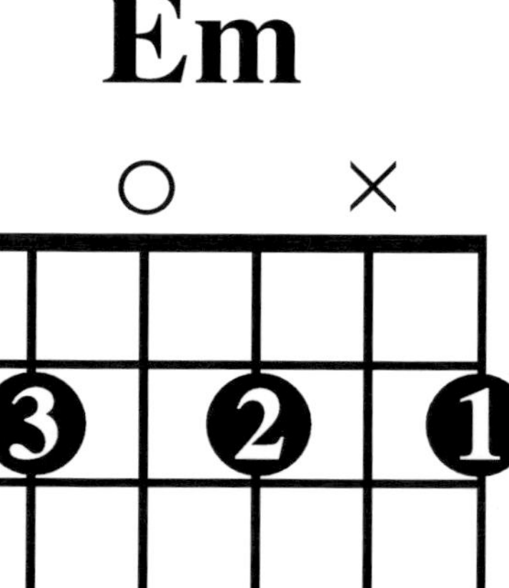

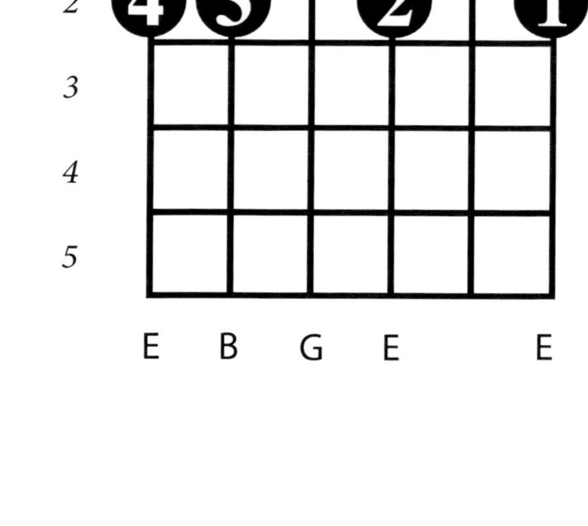

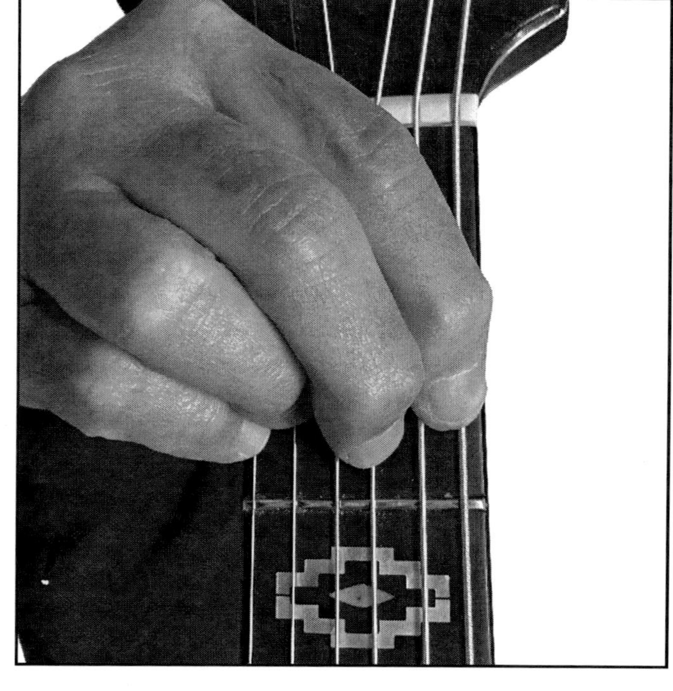

Em7

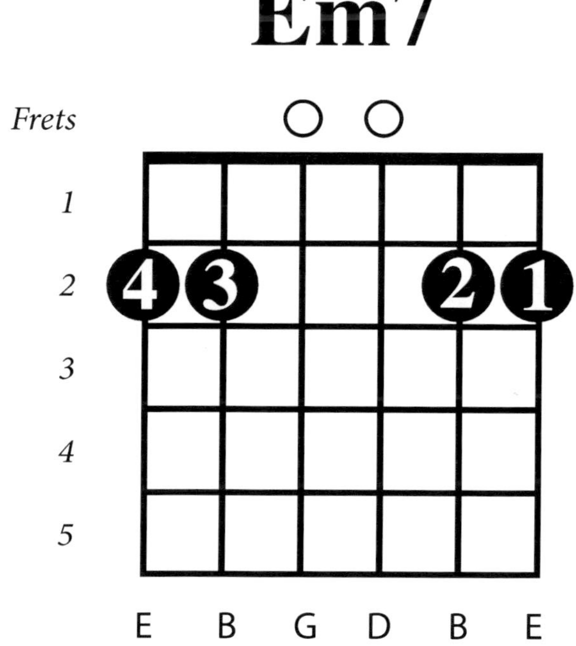

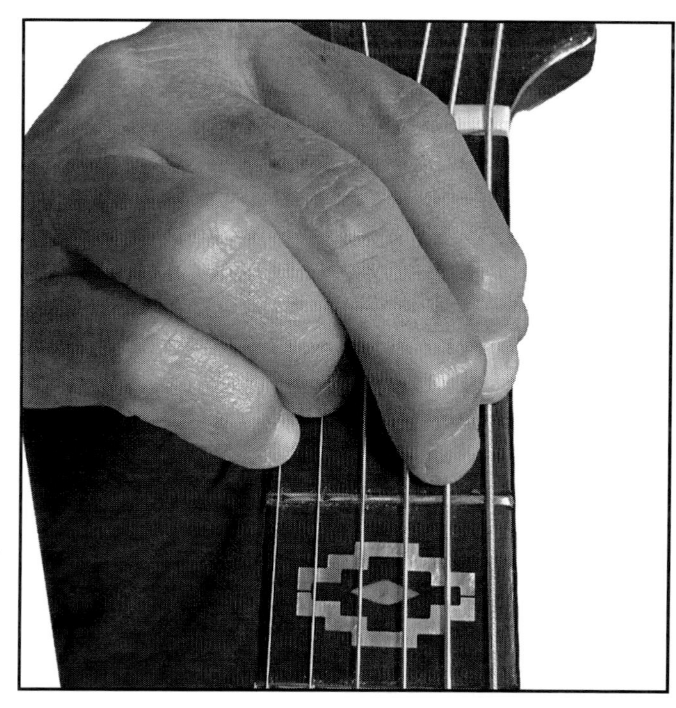

DADGAD

Tuning: **D A D G A D**
Strings: ⑥ ⑤ ④ ③ ② ①

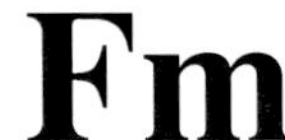

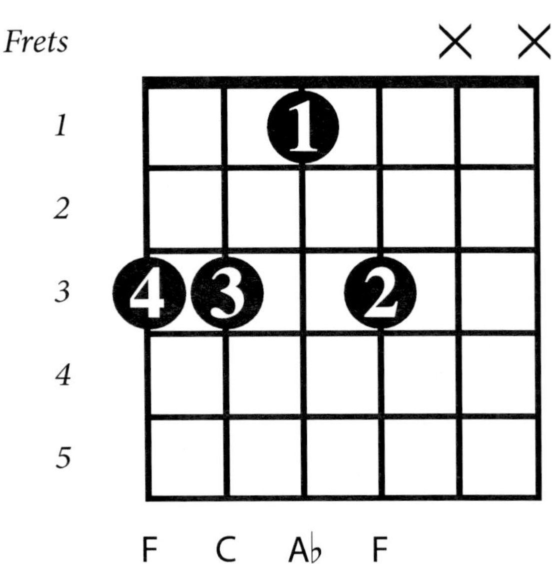

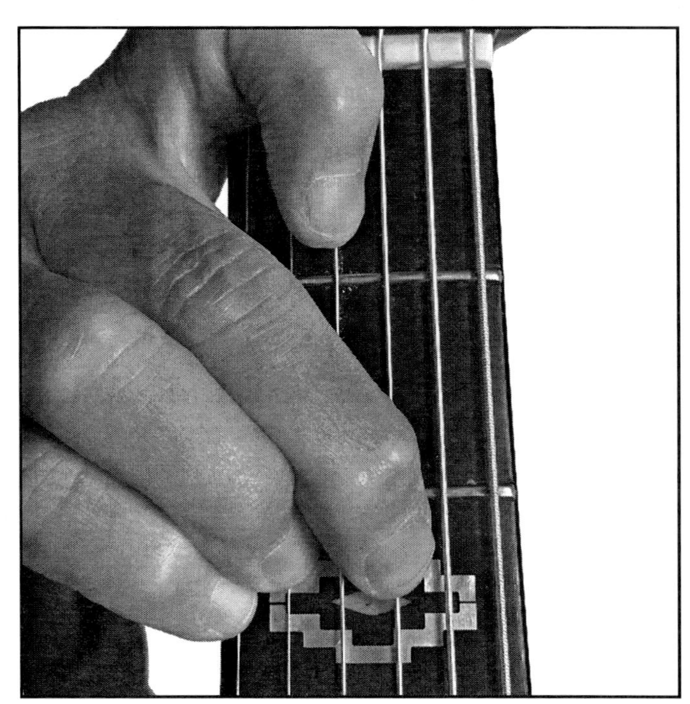

Fm7

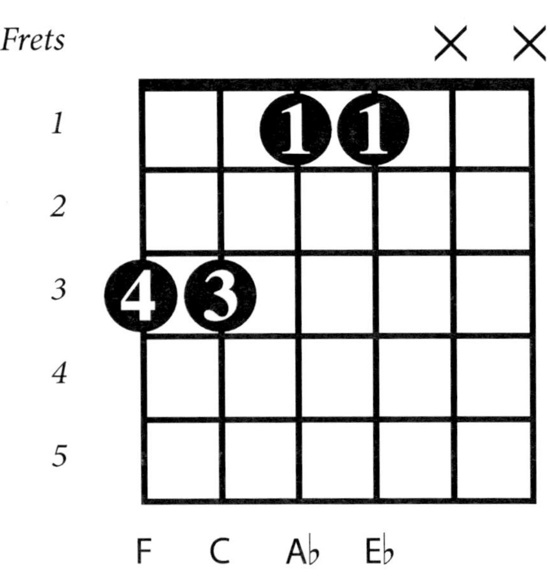

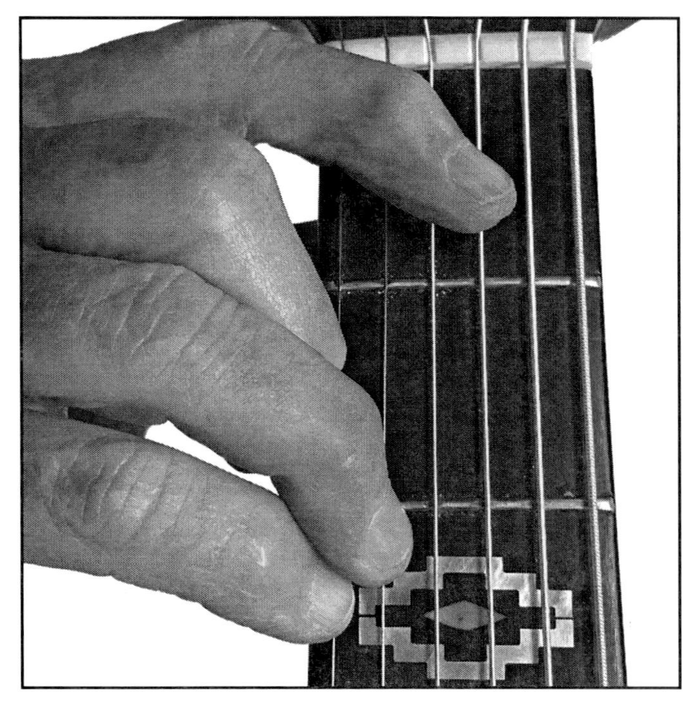

DADGAD

Tuning: **D A D G A D**
Strings: ⑥ ⑤ ④ ③ ② ①

G

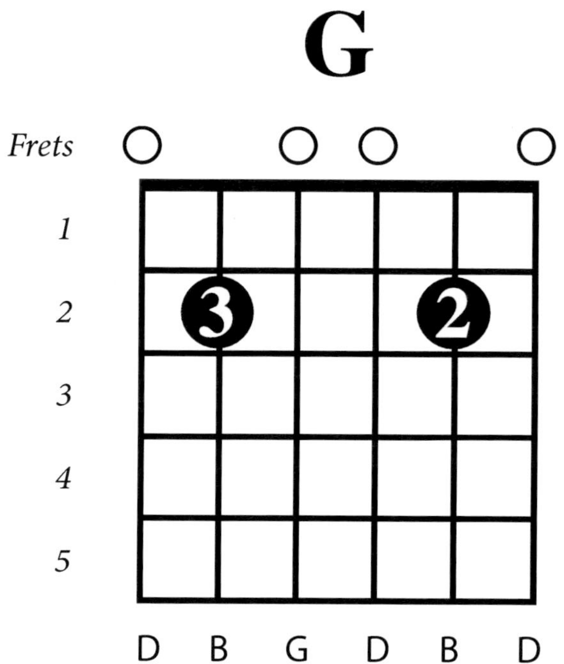

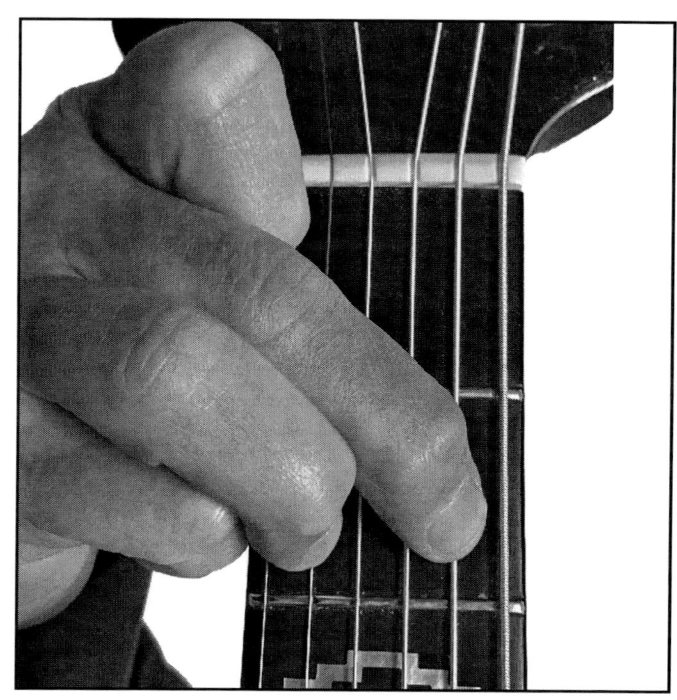

GMaj7

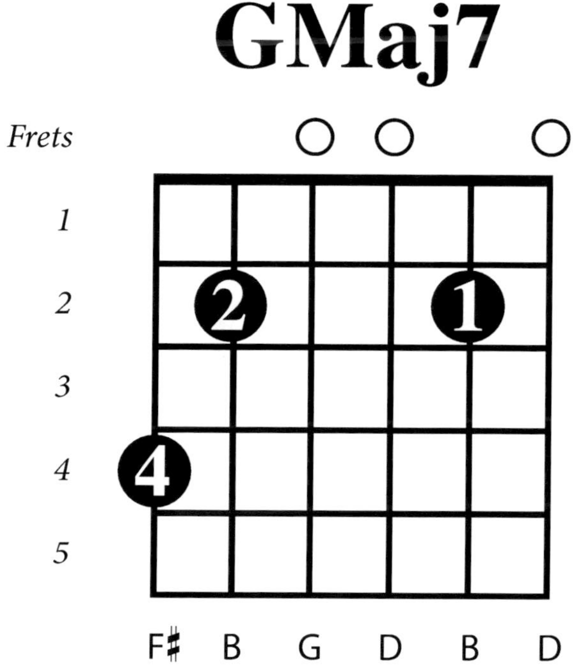

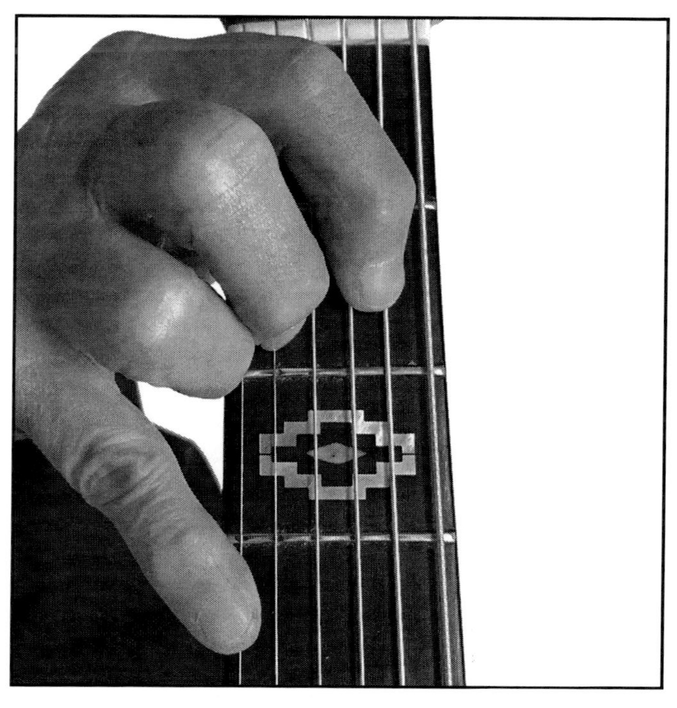

DADGAD

Tuning: **D A D G A D**
Strings: ⑥ ⑤ ④ ③ ② ①

GMaj6

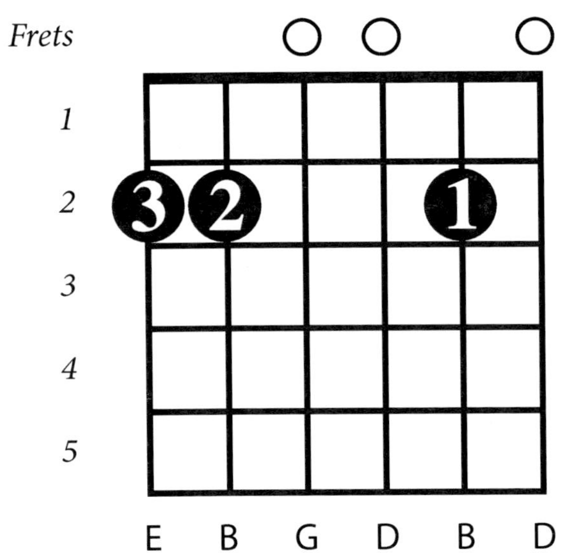

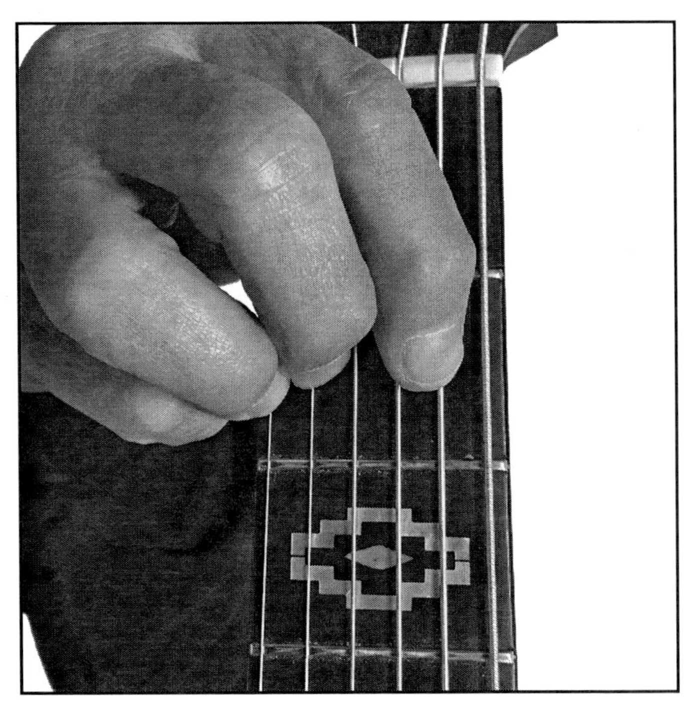

A

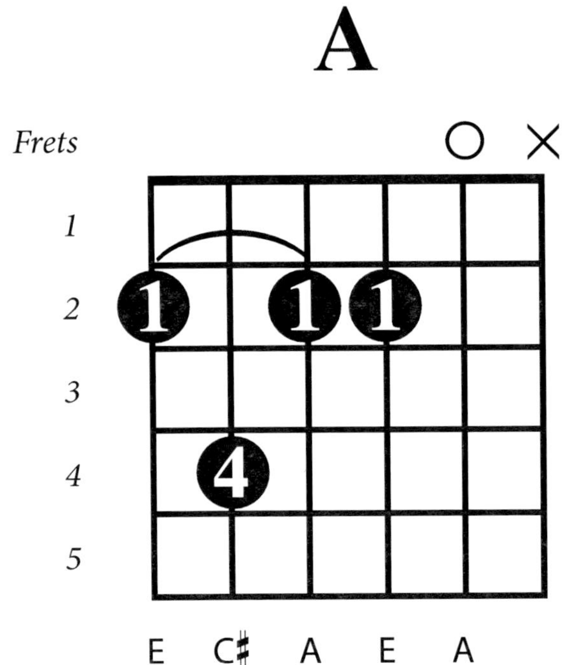

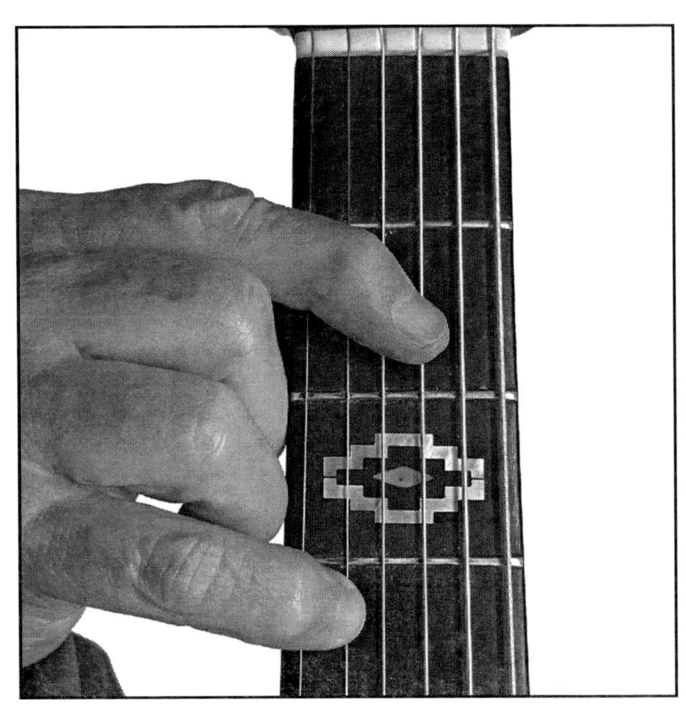

DADGAD

Tuning: **D A D G A D**
Strings: ⑥ ⑤ ④ ③ ② ①

A7

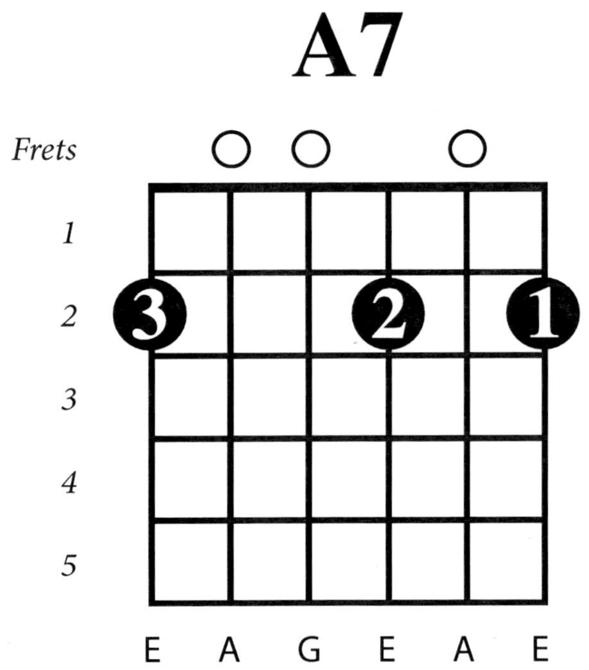

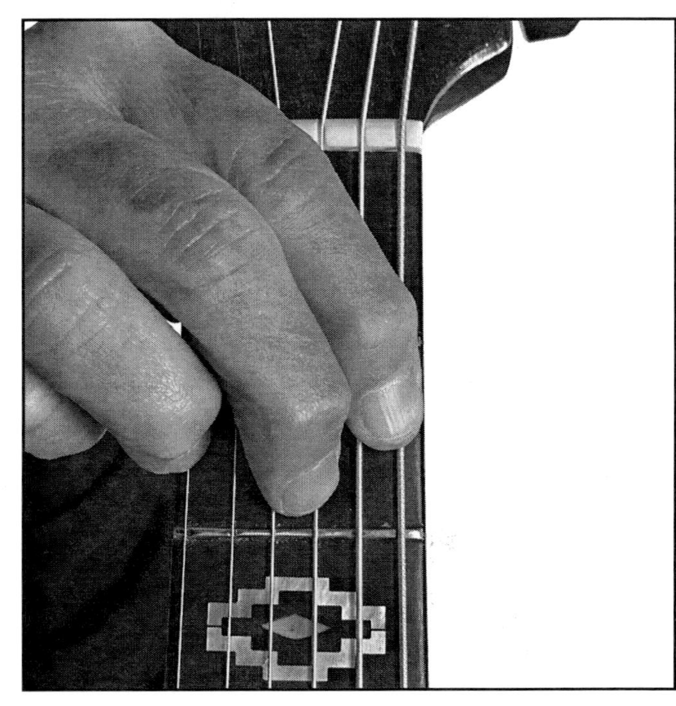

Am7

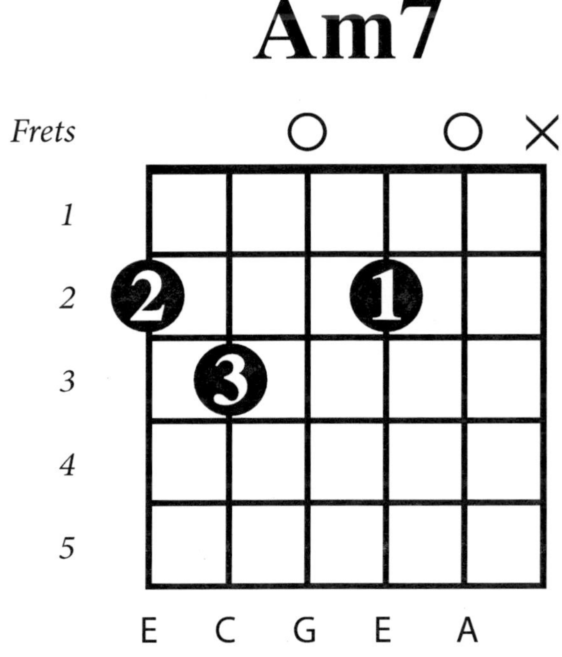

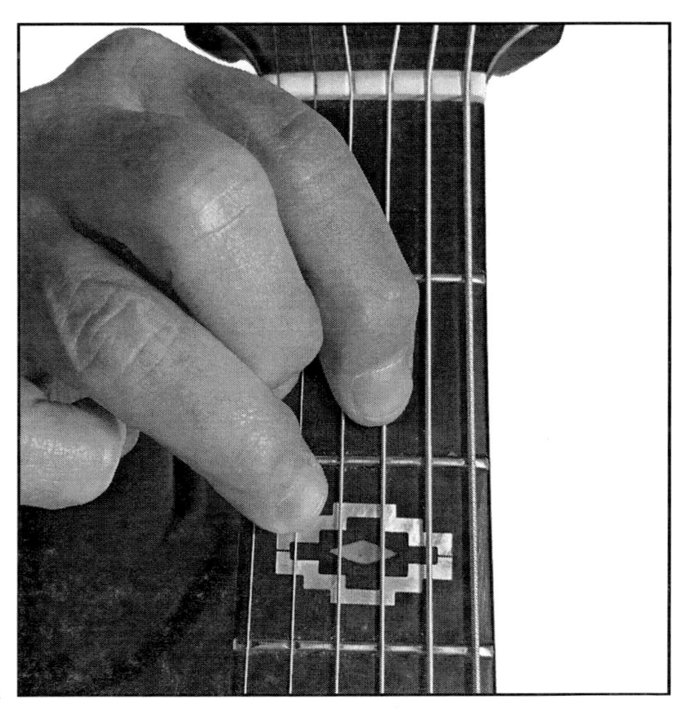

Dropped-D

Tuning: **D A D G B E**
Strings: ⑥ ⑤ ④ ③ ② ①

D

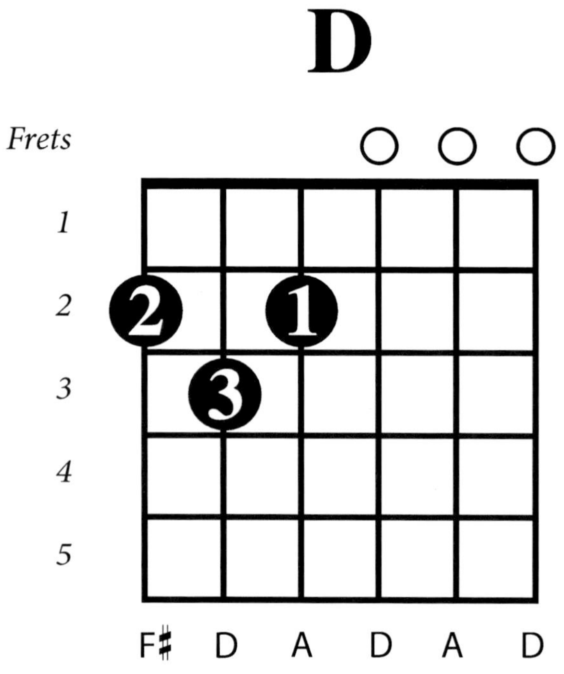

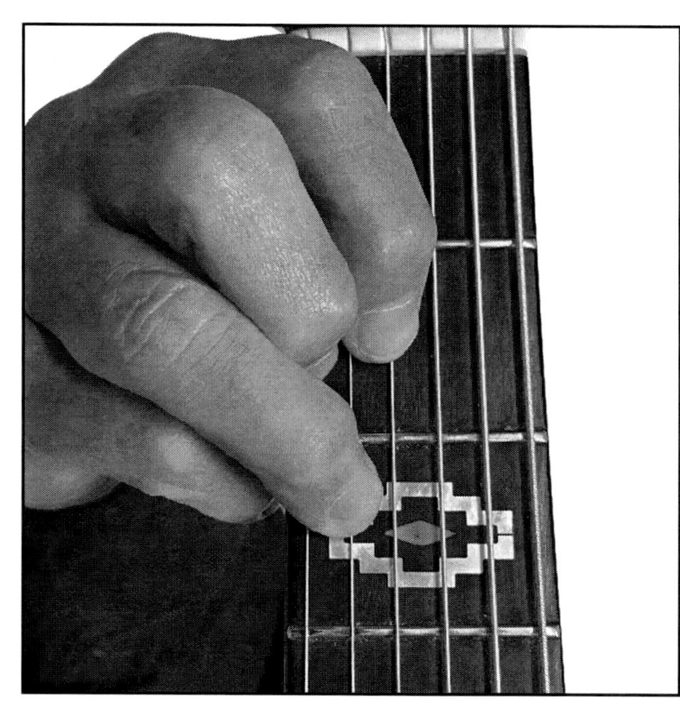

Dm

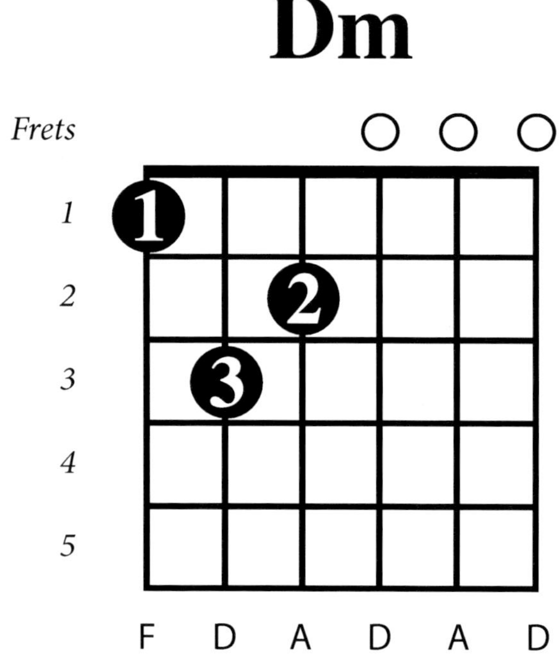

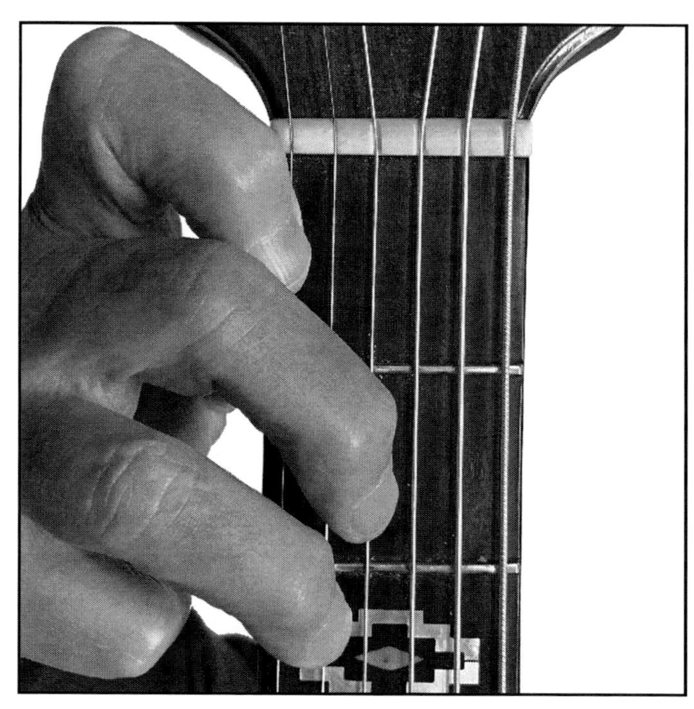

Dropped-D

Tuning: **D A D G B E**
Strings: ⑥ ⑤ ④ ③ ② ①

D7

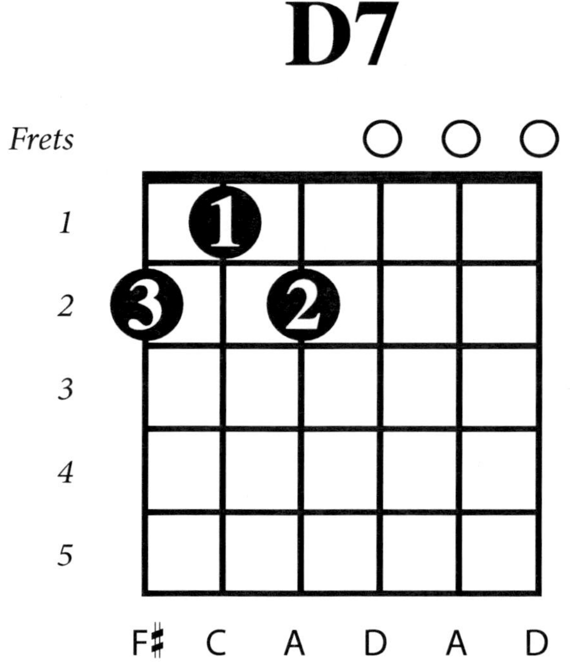

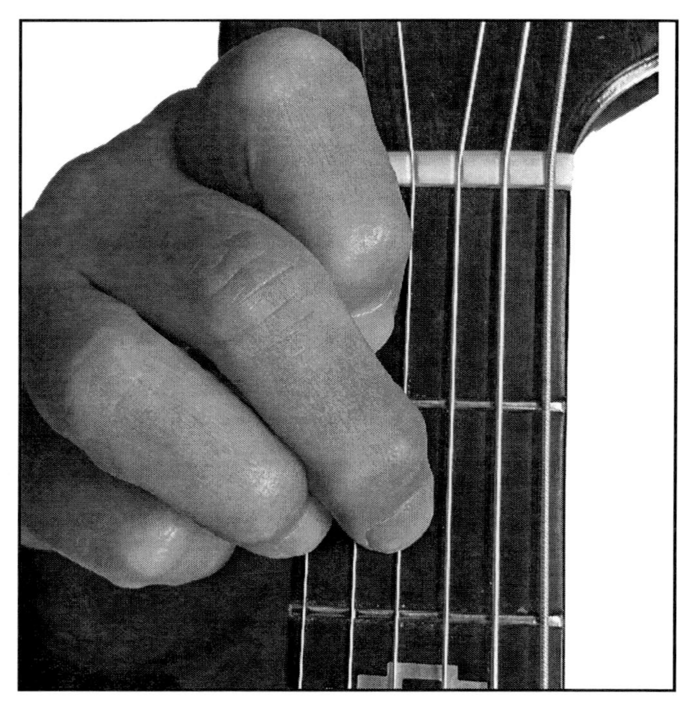

DMaj7

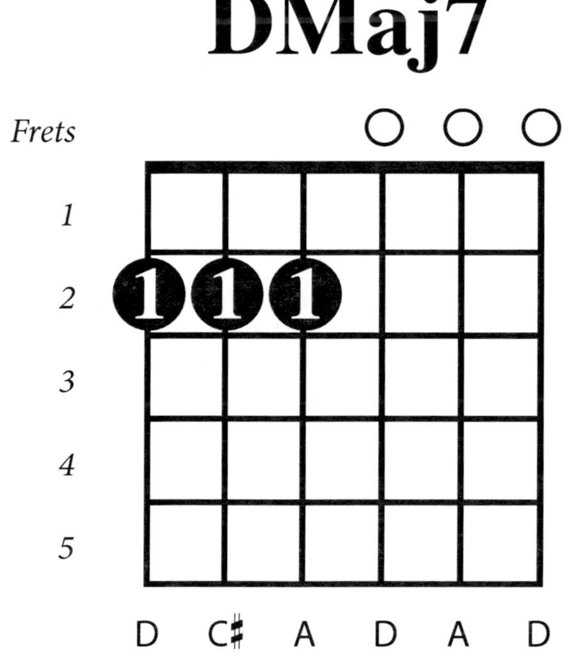

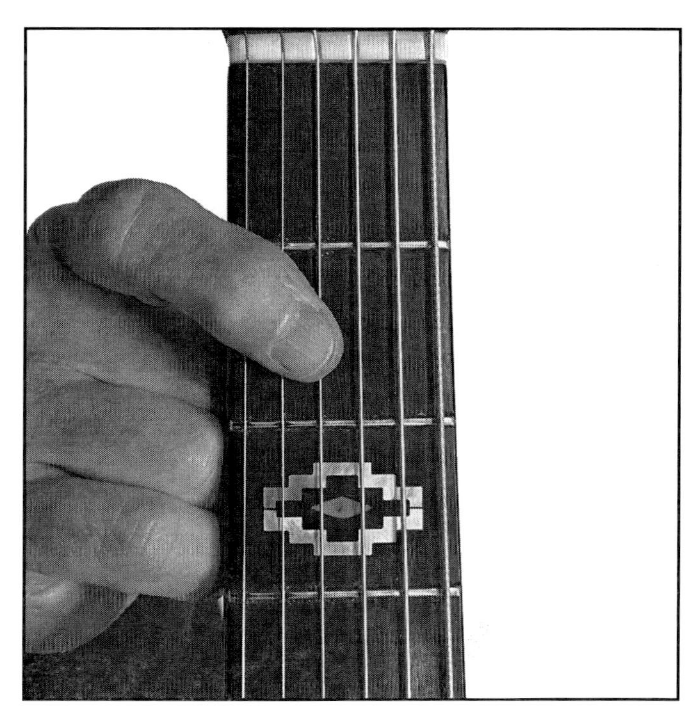

Dropped-D

Tuning: **D A D G B E**
Strings: ⑥ ⑤ ④ ③ ② ①

DMaj6

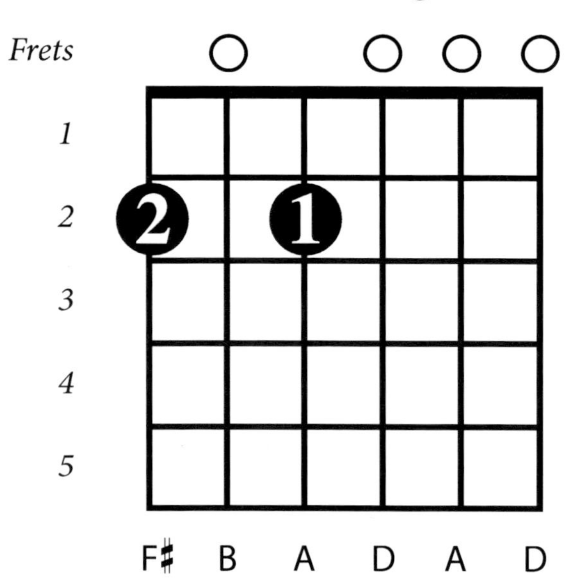

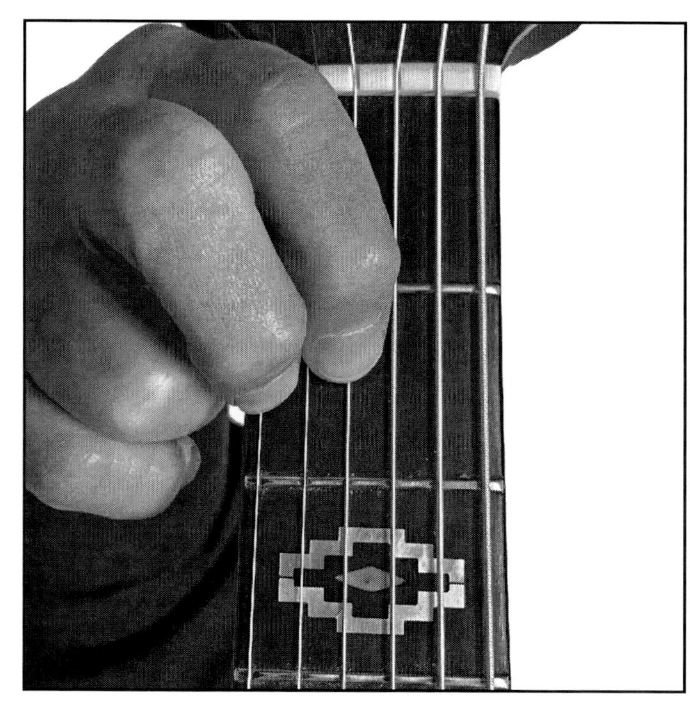

Dm6

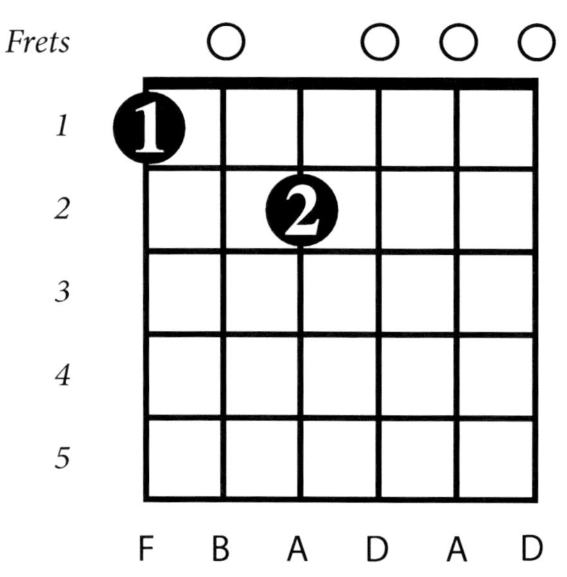

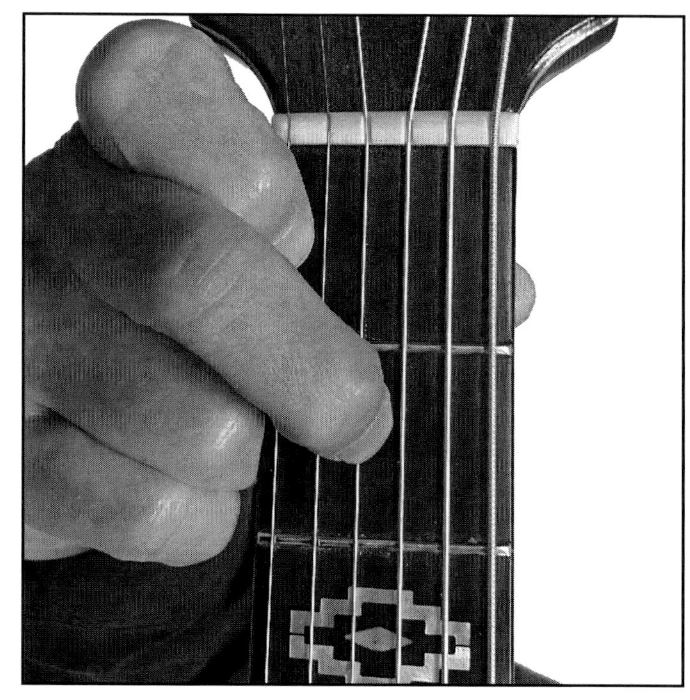

Dropped-D

Tuning: **D A D G B E**
Strings: ⑥ ⑤ ④ ③ ② ①

Dm7

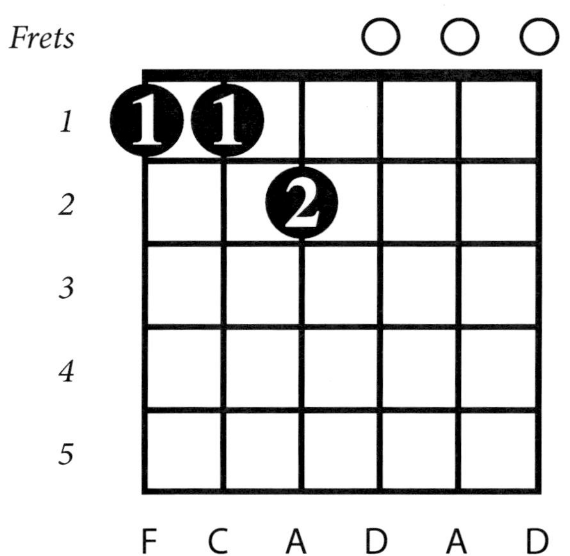

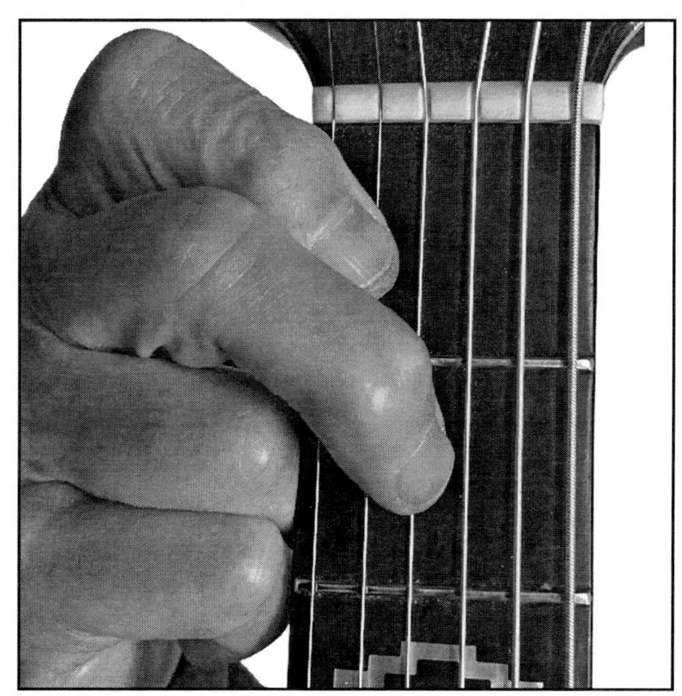

Dm-Maj7

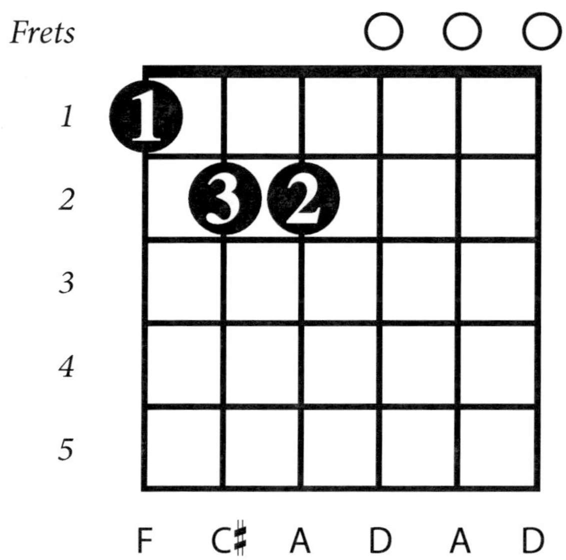

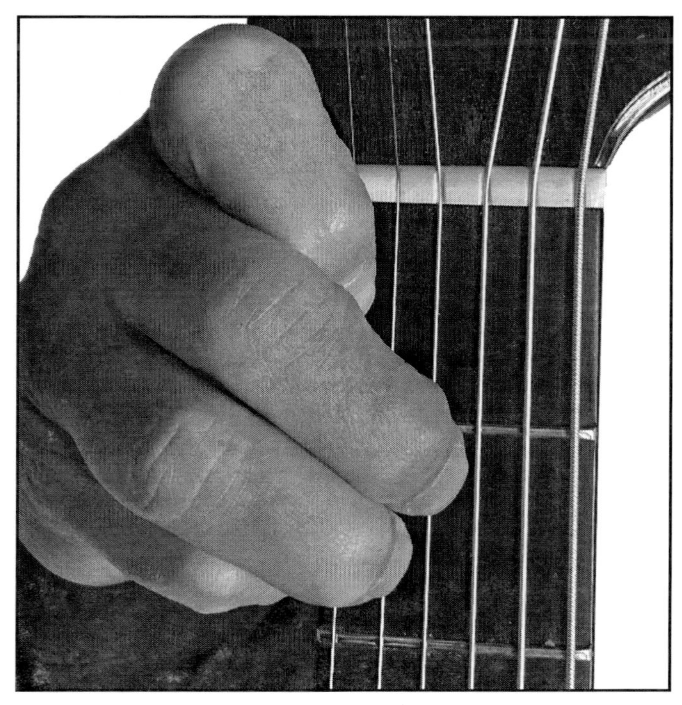

Dropped-D

Tuning: **D A D G B E**
Strings: ⑥ ⑤ ④ ③ ② ①

D add9

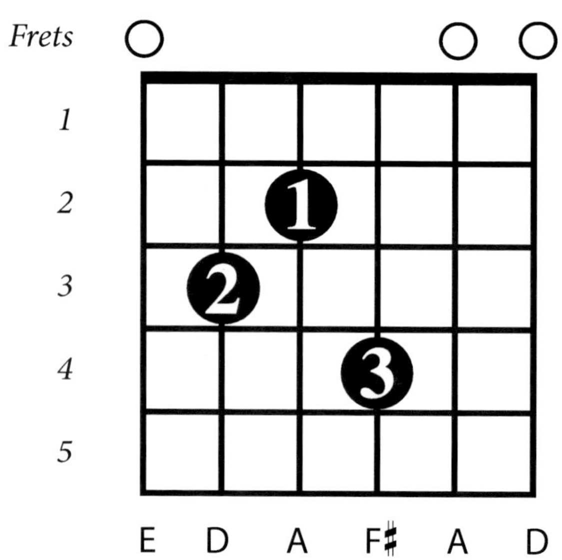

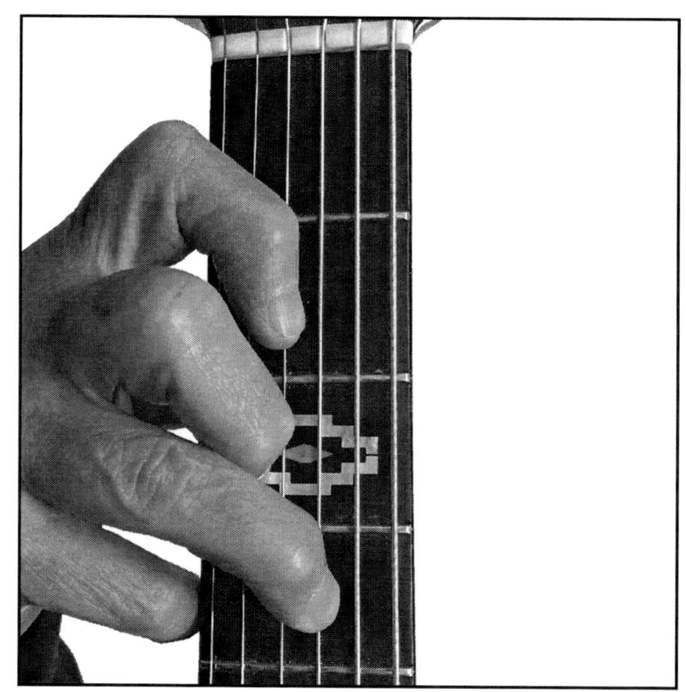

Dm add9

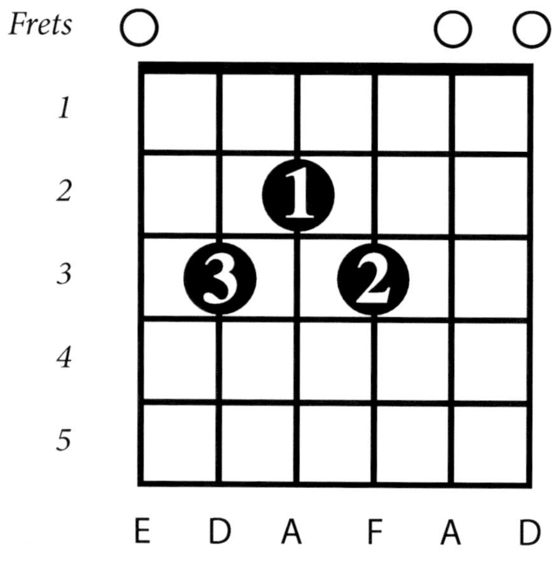

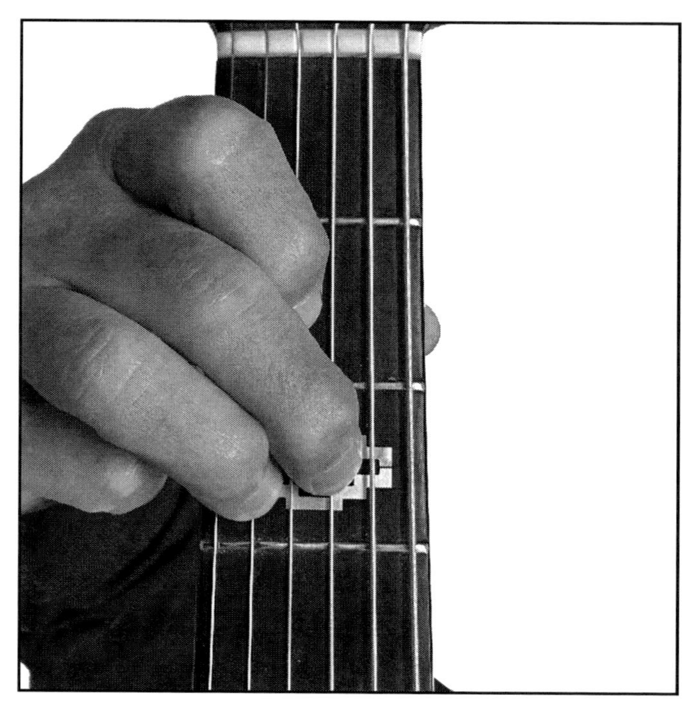

Dropped-D

Tuning: **D A D G B E**
Strings: ⑥ ⑤ ④ ③ ② ①

Dsus

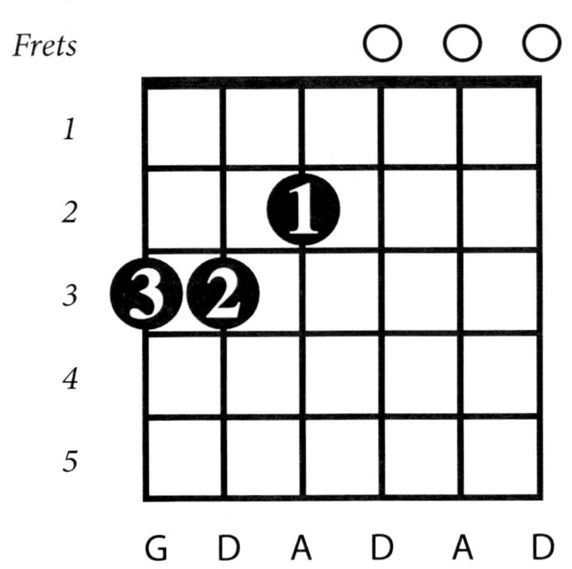

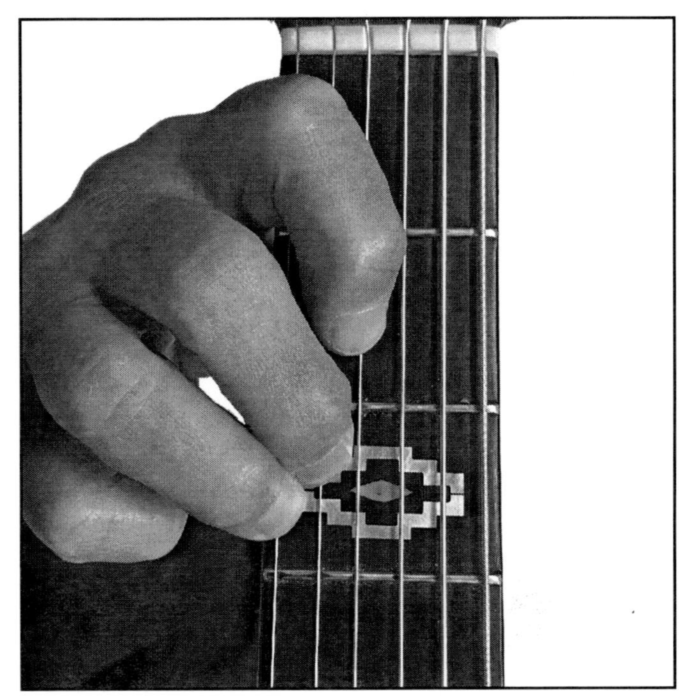

DMaj7 add6

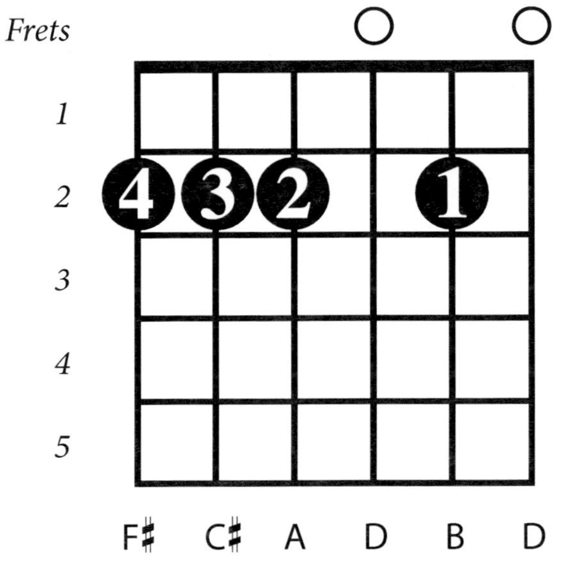

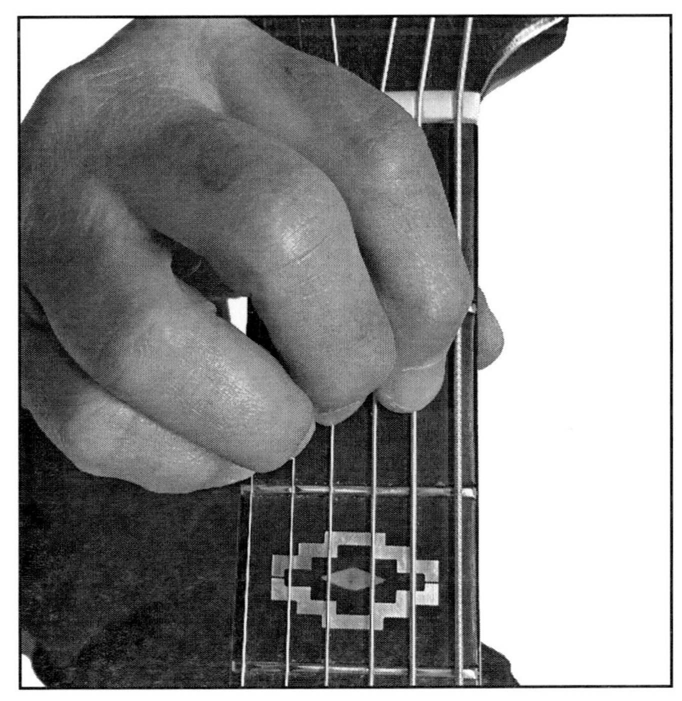

Dropped-D

Tuning: **D A D G B E**

Strings: **⑥ ⑤ ④ ③ ② ①**

DMaj9

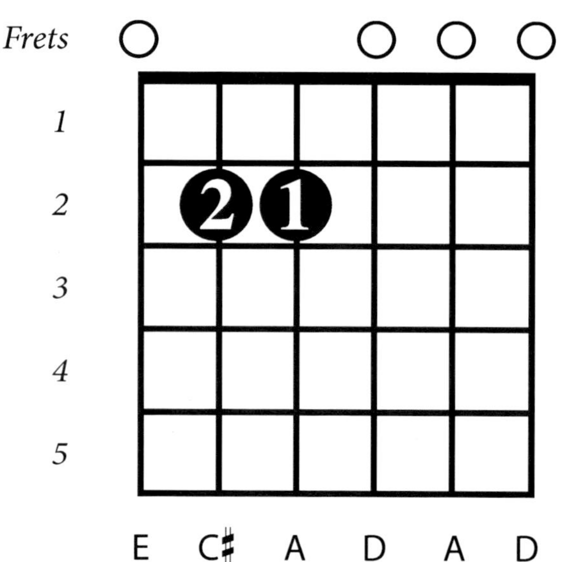

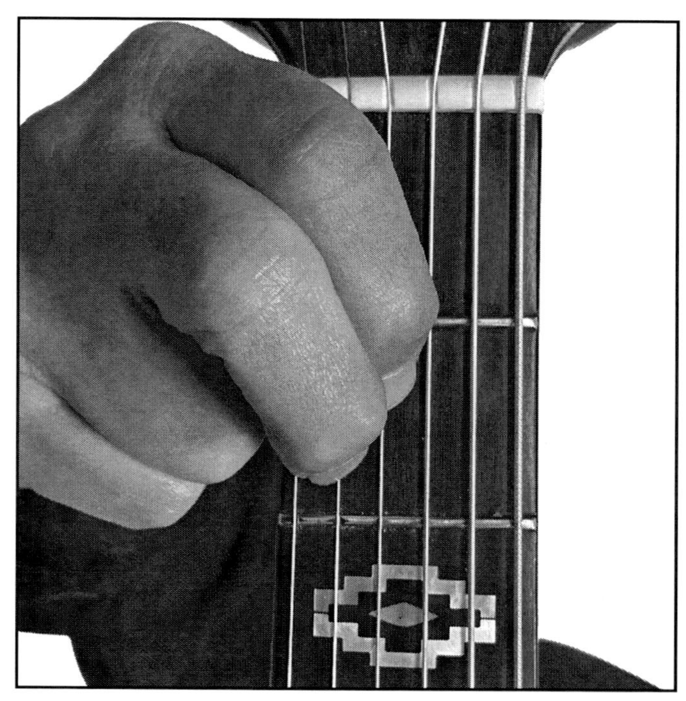

DMaj13

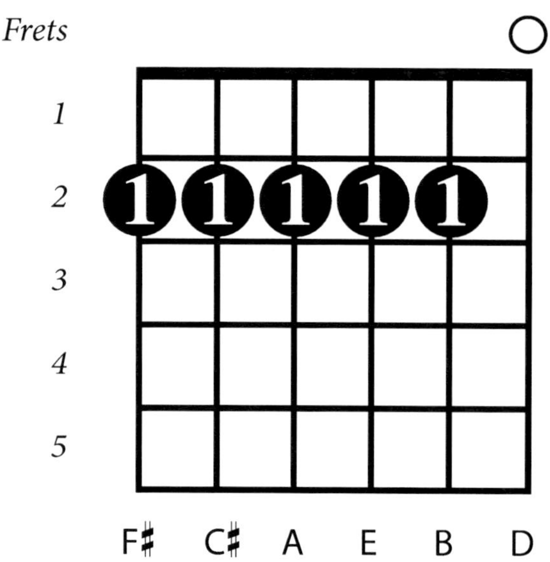

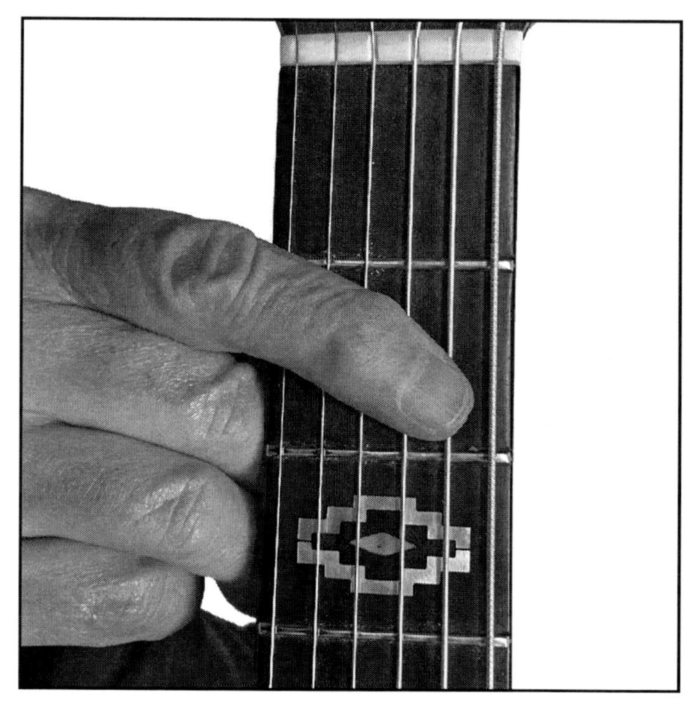

Dropped-D

Tuning: D A D G B E
Strings: ⑥ ⑤ ④ ③ ② ①

D6/9

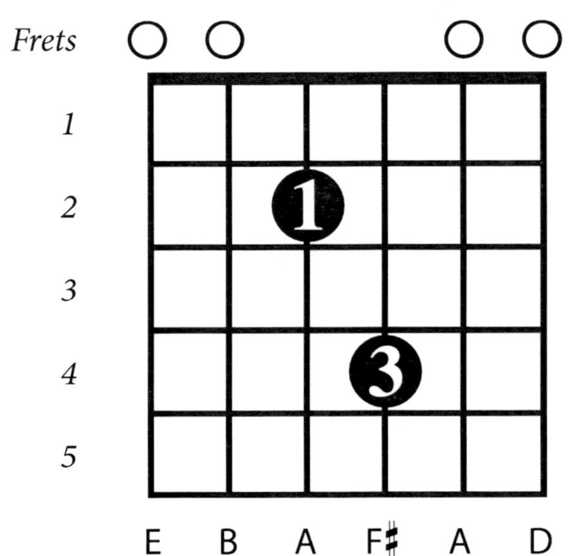

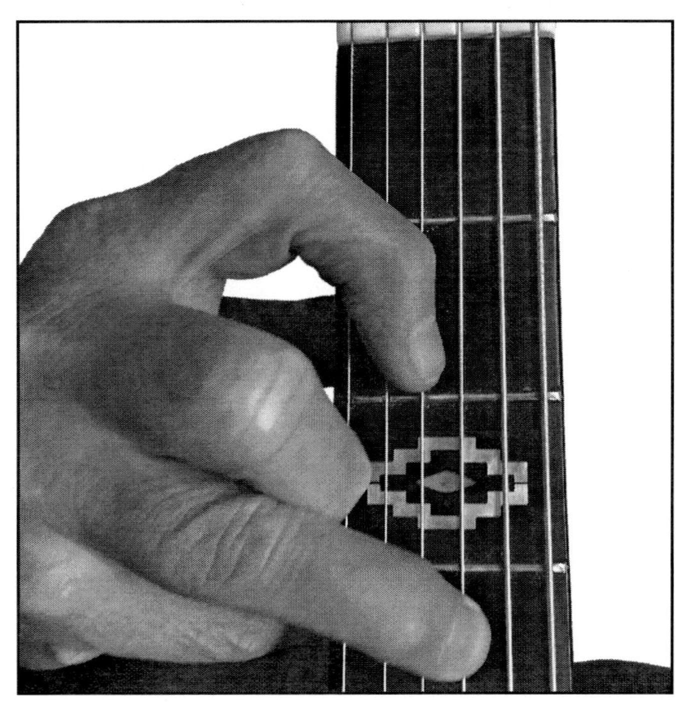

D°

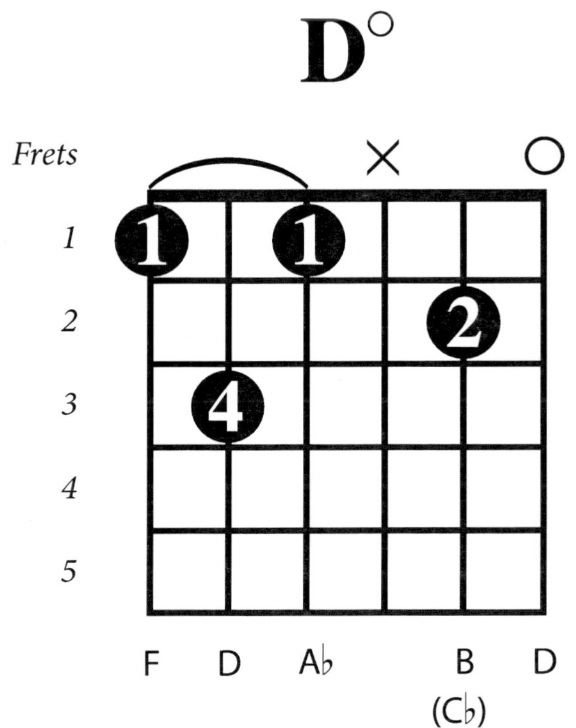

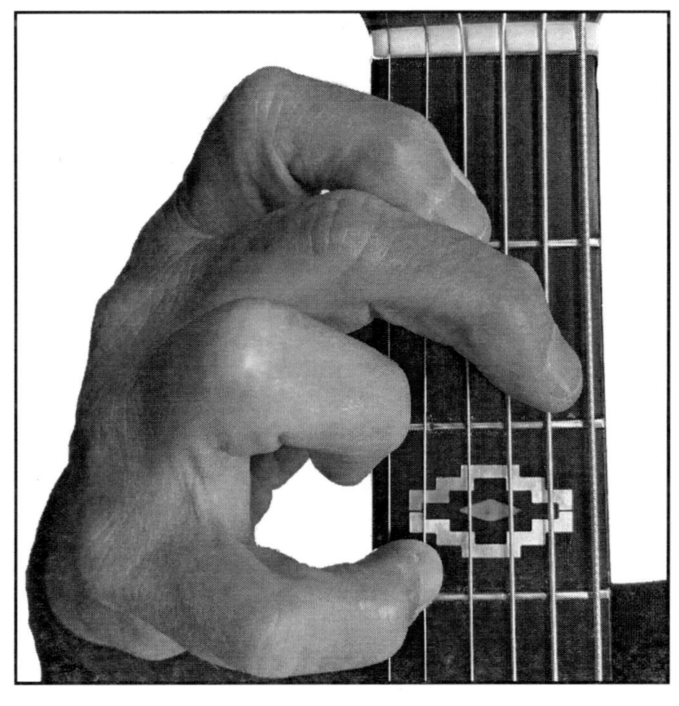

Dropped-D

Tuning: **D A D G B E**
Strings: ⑥ ⑤ ④ ③ ② ①

Em

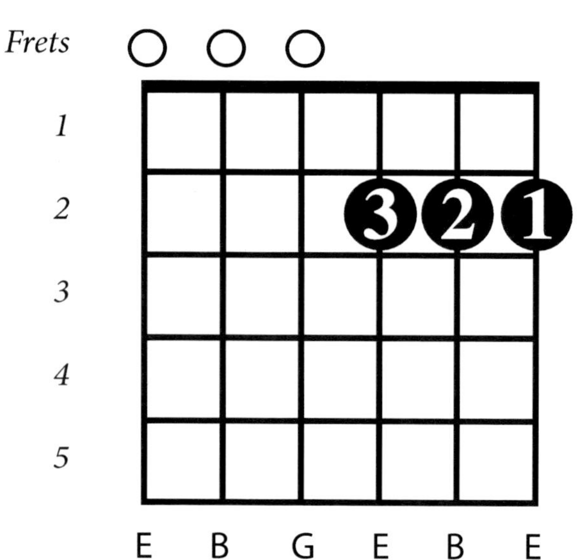

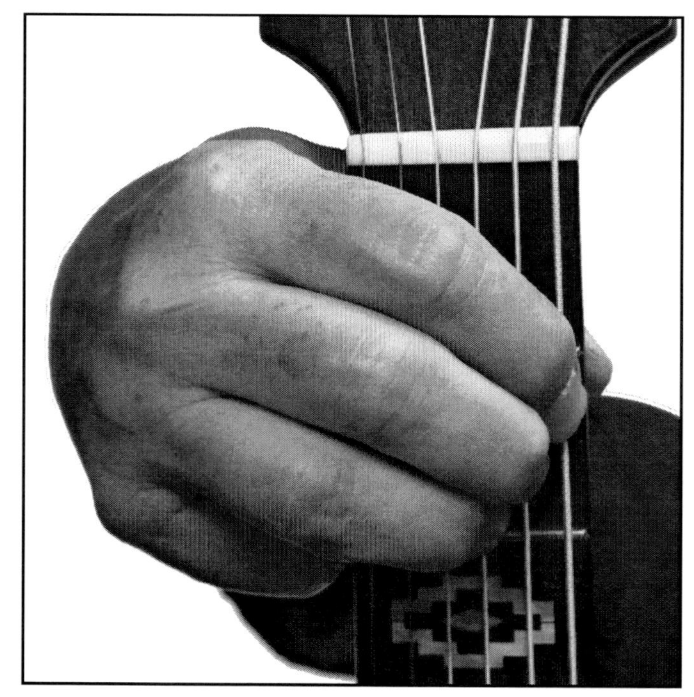

Em7

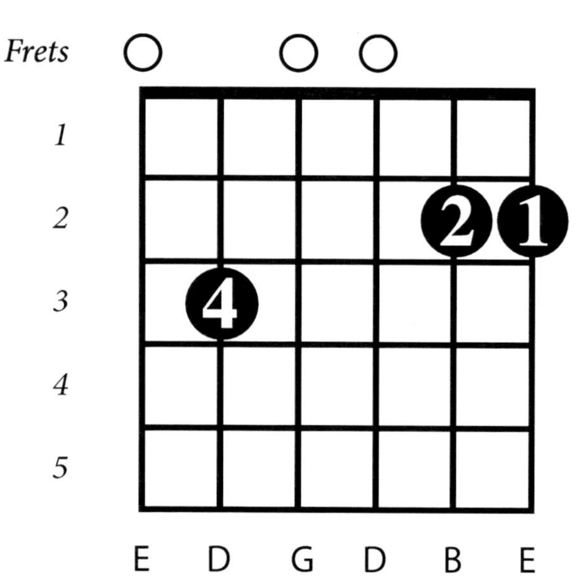

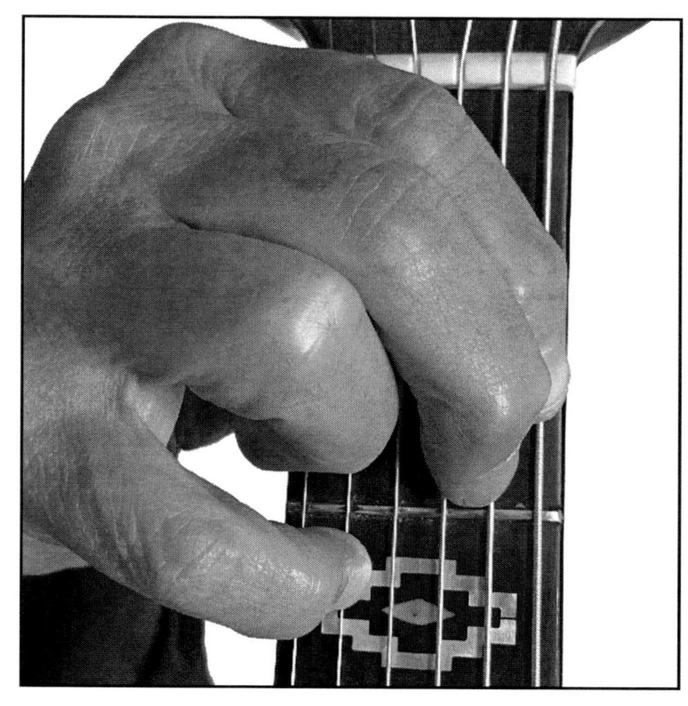

Dropped-D

Tuning: **D A D G B E**

Strings: ⑥ ⑤ ④ ③ ② ①

Fm

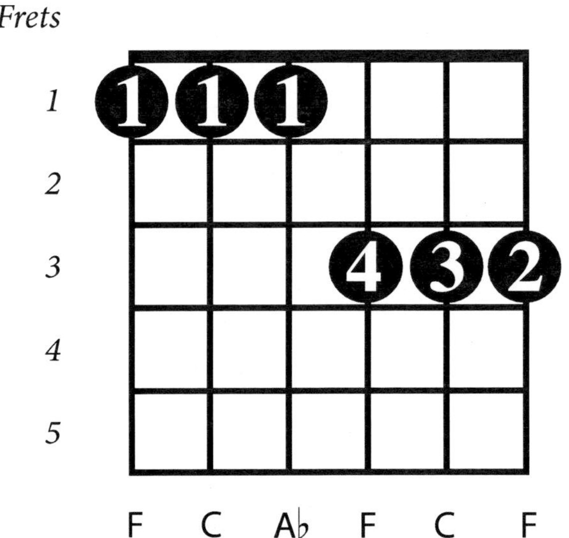

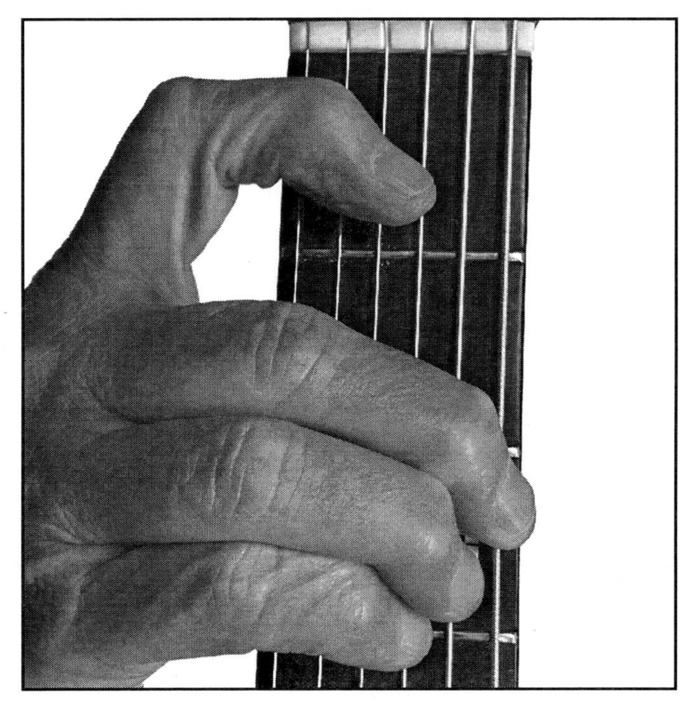

Fm7

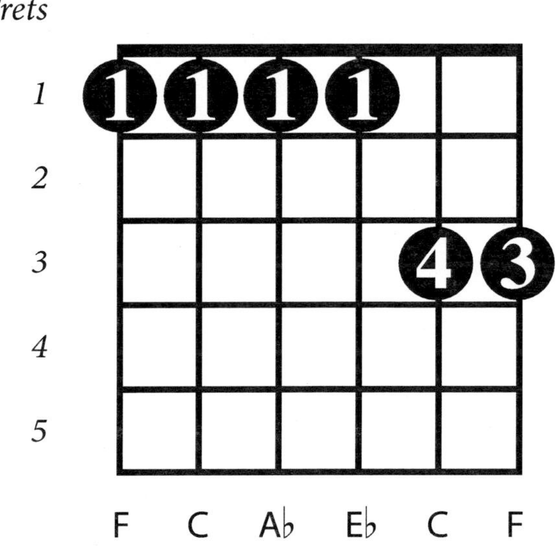

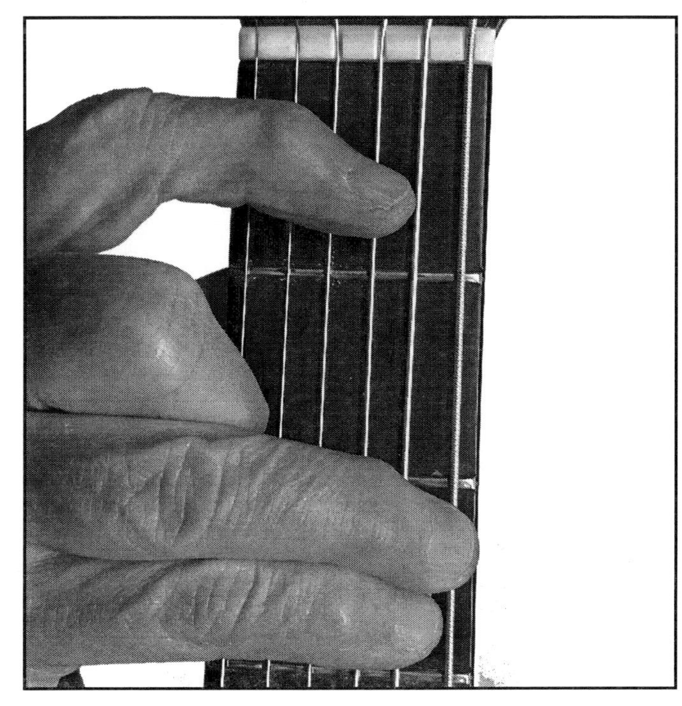

Dropped-D

Tuning: **D A D G B E**
Strings: ⑥ ⑤ ④ ③ ② ①

G

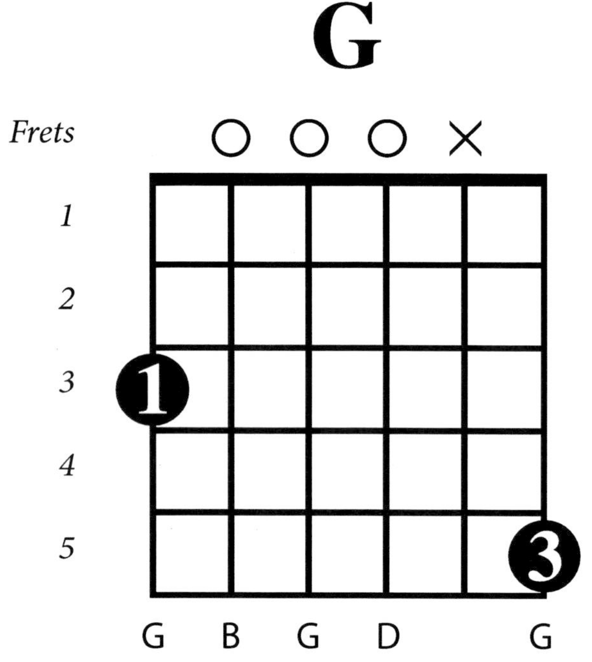

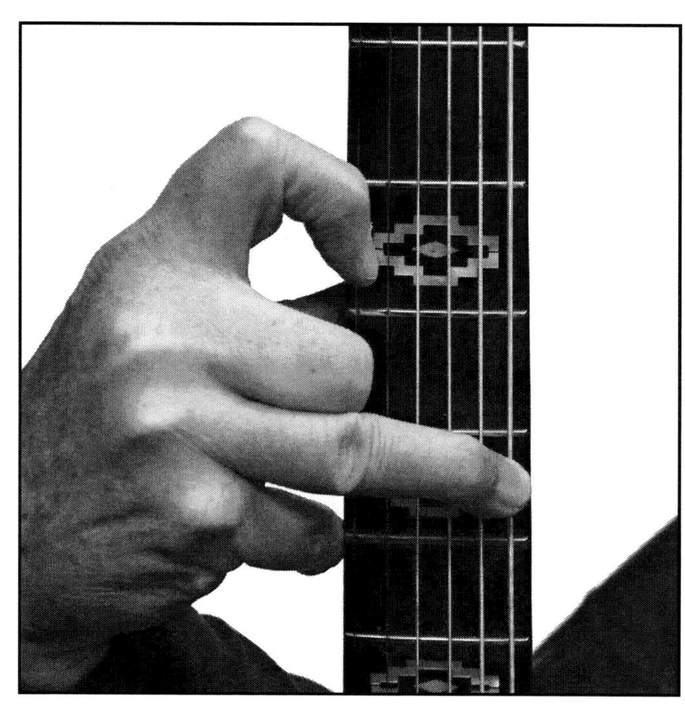

GMaj7

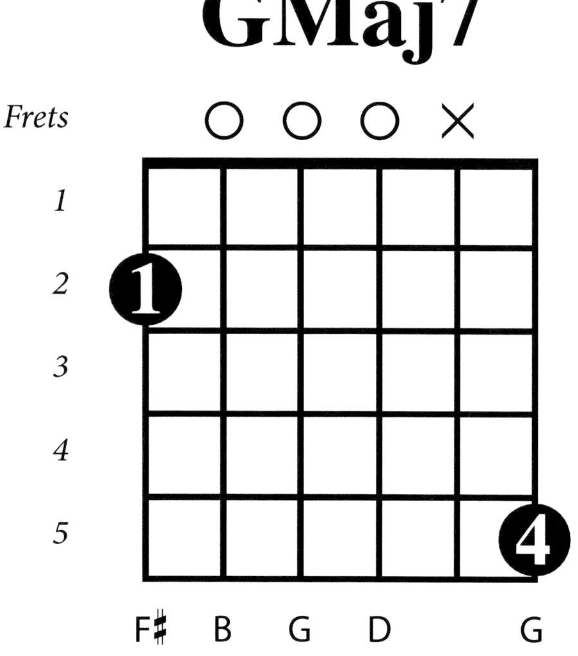

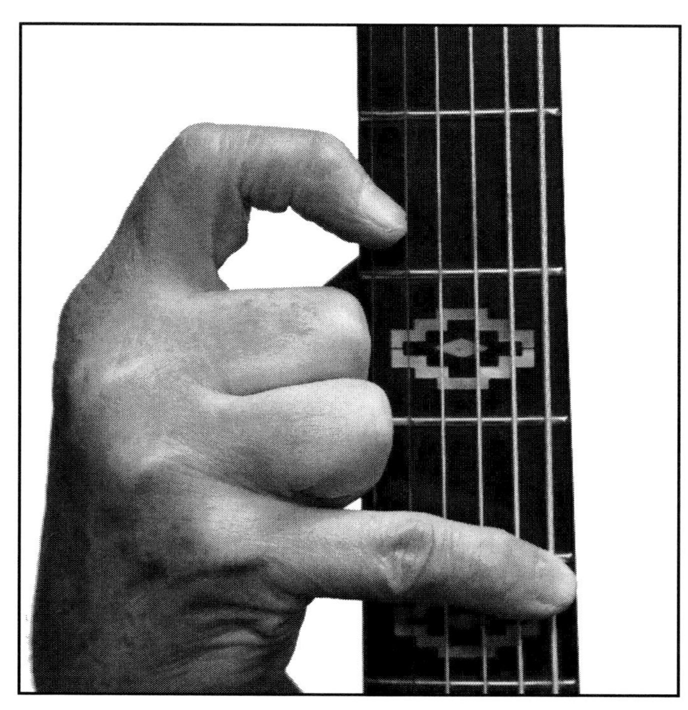

Dropped-D

Tuning: **D A D G B E**

Strings: ⑥ ⑤ ④ ③ ② ①

GMaj6

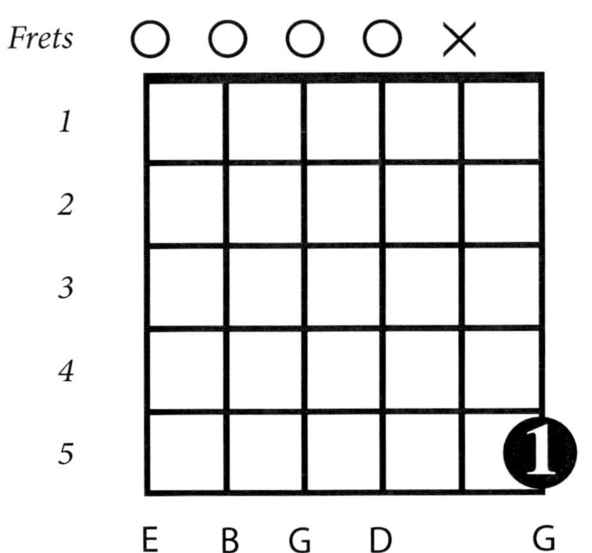

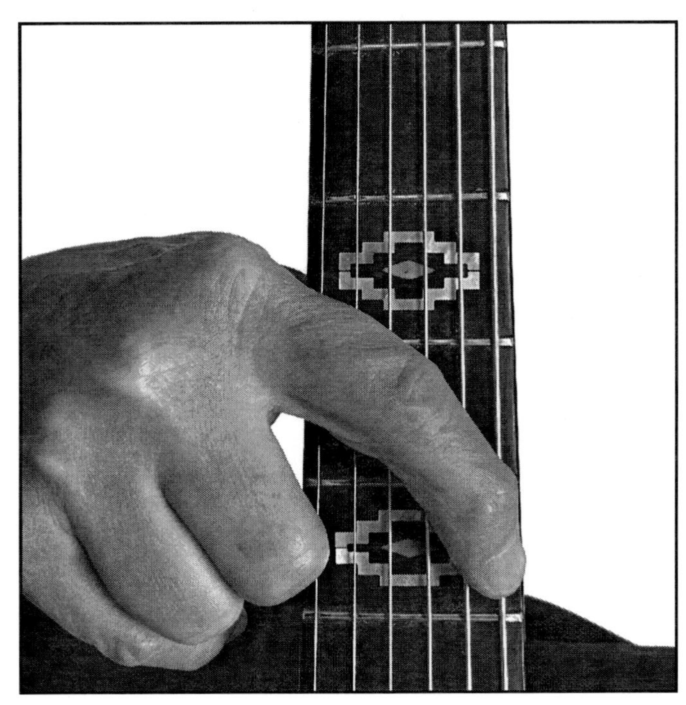

Gm7

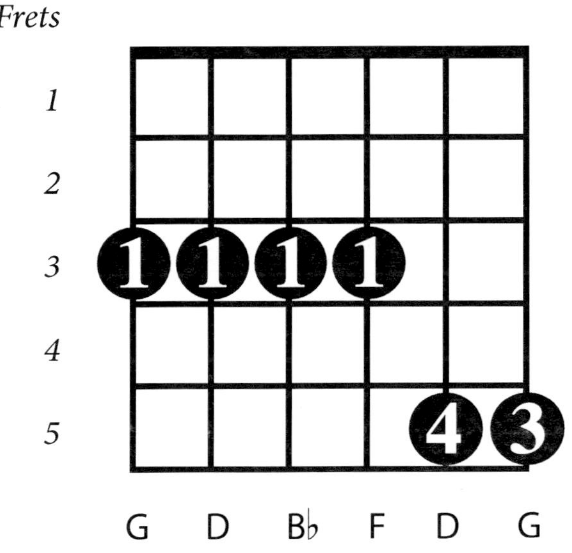

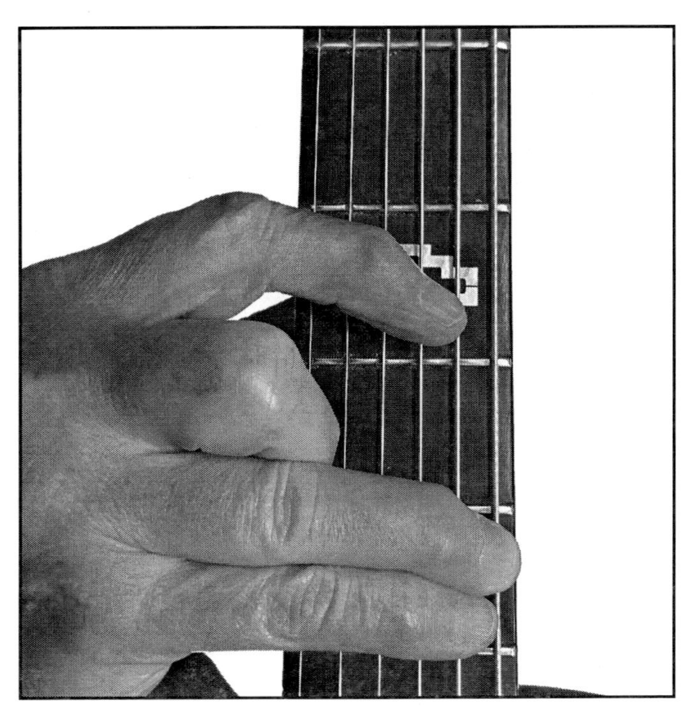

Dropped-D

Tuning: **D A D G B E**
Strings: ⑥ ⑤ ④ ③ ② ①

G6/9

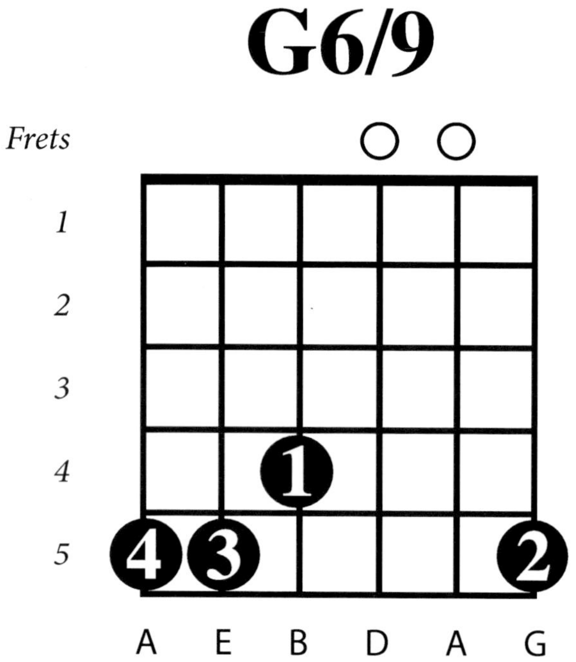

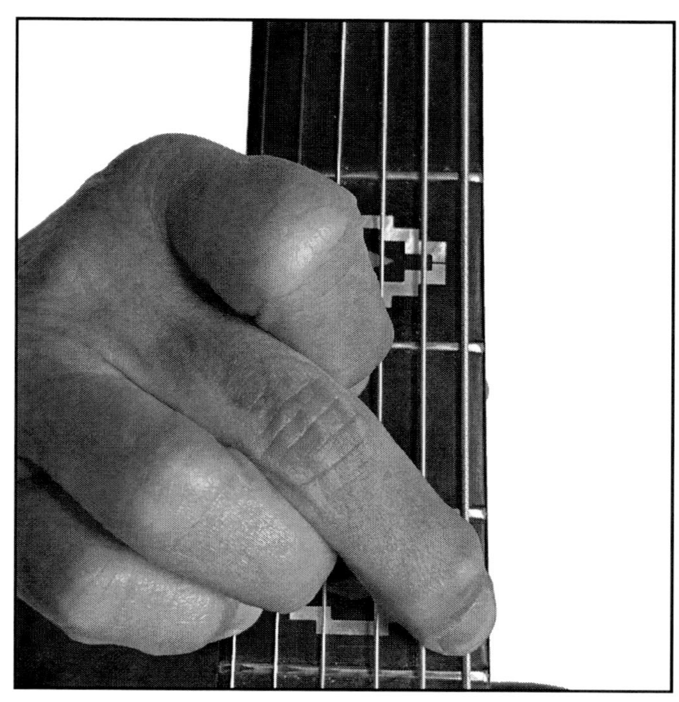

GMaj9

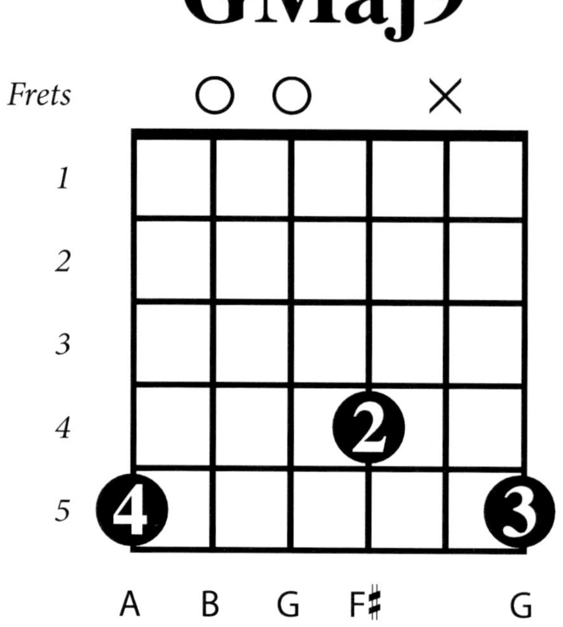

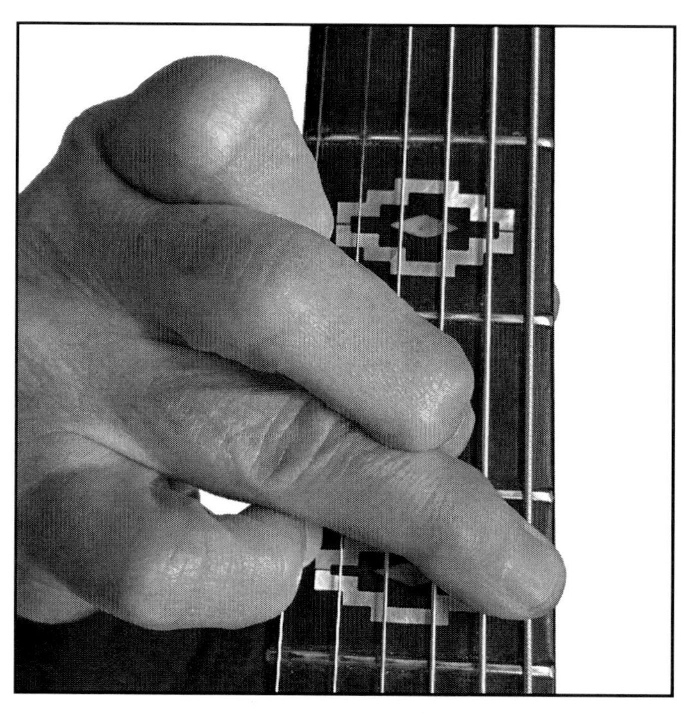